Amanda de Lima Martins

Rural territorial development

Amanda de Lima Martins

Rural territorial development

Potential and limits of induced territories in Brazil

ScienciaScripts

Imprint
Any brand names and product names mentioned in this book are subject to trademark, brand or patent protection and are trademarks or registered trademarks of their respective holders. The use of brand names, product names, common names, trade names, product descriptions etc. even without a particular marking in this work is in no way to be construed to mean that such names may be regarded as unrestricted in respect of trademark and brand protection legislation and could thus be used by anyone.

Cover image: www.ingimage.com

This book is a translation from the original published under ISBN 978-3-330-76774-4.

Publisher:
Sciencia Scripts
is a trademark of
Dodo Books Indian Ocean Ltd. and OmniScriptum S.R.L publishing group

120 High Road, East Finchley, London, N2 9ED, United Kingdom
Str. Armeneasca 28/1, office 1, Chisinau MD-2012, Republic of Moldova, Europe
Managing Directors: Ieva Konstantinova, Victoria Ursu
info@omniscriptum.com

Printed at: see last page
ISBN: 978-620-8-57577-9

To Minas Gerais and the people of Minas Gerais, the fighting and loving people who welcomed me in a special way.

ACKNOWLEDGEMENTS

To my parents, who at all times encouraged me with love and affection and made me believe that there are no challenges so great that they can't be overcome.

To Nádia and Larissa, more than just sorority friends, they were my real family in Uberlândia, a true marriage, in which our daily contact did not deconstruct our friendship and companionship, but only strengthened it.

To my fellow fighters, Agnes, Jaqueline, Núbia, Paula and Priscila, and to the student movement, for the moments of collective growth, the laughter and the crises, without ever abandoning our ideal, a classless society, without exploiters and exploited.

To Ada Luisa, for her faithful and true friendship, for the moments of being a mum and a sister, no amount of thanks can express all that I owe her.

To the 48th class, who made the academic burden lighter, among them those who were part of two administrations of the Academic Directory with me, in which we experienced moments of political maturity.

To Prof Dr Antônio César Ortega, my scientific initiation and monograph supervisor, who was always willing to help me with my work and even advise me on academic life.

To ProP. DP. Ana Paula Avellar, for guiding me through the Institutional Undergraduate Teaching Scholarship Programme in the early years of my degree, when I could count on all her experience to help me set up various activities. For her co-operation as Course Co-ordinator, with the Academic Directory, in the administrations I took part in, and also for her help and encouragement in carrying out the exchange programme with Portugal.

To Prof Soraia Aparecida Cardozo Soraia Aparecida Cardozo, for giving me the opportunity to tutor Brazilian Economics I and for her always critical and inspiring lessons.

To the other professors and staff at the Institute of Economics, who contributed directly or indirectly to my academic training, especially Maura and Sirlene, who helped me so many times.

To the Federal University of Uberlândia, for the great opportunities it has offered me, through the conviviality and discussions with excellent teachers and students in its various spaces, providing me with unrivalled maturity.

SUMMARY

INTRODUCTION

In order to boost the development of municipalities with low socio-economic levels, in a context of unequal economic growth, the federal government has implemented policies to induce socio-productive arrangements throughout the country. This is a trend that began with the emergence of decentralised policies at the end of the 20th century, in which sub-national areas became the focus of public policies. Development policies with a rural territorial focus deserve special mention, as they manage to incorporate innovative factors.

As part of these policies, the Rural Territories were created, using the Intermunicipal Consortia for Sustainable Rural Development as a reference, as part of the Infrastructure and Services line of PRONAF (National Programme for Strengthening Family Farming). These new territorial spaces were set up with some innovative aspects, such as: the territorial focus, the extrapolation of municipal boundaries, the distinctive vision between rural and agricultural, the strategy of overcoming the rural-urban dichotomy, the attempt to build a territorial pact that would overcome open intra- and inter-class conflicts and, finally, to generate an incentive for development. There are currently 164 territories across Brazil.

With similar objectives, but focused specifically on food security and income generation, Intermunicipal Consortia for Food Security and Local Development (CONSADs) have been set up as part of the Ministry of Social Development and Fight against Hunger's (MDS) strategy to generate work and income opportunities in the country's peripheral sub-regions. This strategy works through structural changes on a social and economic level, falling within the scope of the structural objectives pursued by the Zero Hunger Programme. To this end, 40 CONSADs were set up in 2003, spread across 26 Brazilian states, involving 576 municipalities and a population of approximately 10.5 million inhabitants.

The most recent policy to adopt a territorial approach to rural areas is the Territories of Citizenship. It involves 22 ministries and federal bodies carrying out integrated actions with the aim of overcoming rural poverty and regional inequalities. In addition to the federal government's actions, state and municipal governments are also involved in this project. This induction policy began in 2008 with 60 territories; in 2009 another 60 territories were added, and the 120 territories overlap with the Rural Territories. In 2009, the 120 Citizenship Territories already covered 33% of the municipalities and 23% of the Brazilian population.

Inducing the creation of spaces for territorial agreement with a view to the development of depressed territories is the central feature of these programmes. Therefore, given the weight of their implementation throughout the country, the participation of the three spheres of government (federal, state and municipal) and the participation of civil society make it relevant to study territorial development in Brazil.

There is growing state action through public policies that explore the notion of territorial development beyond the municipalities. The budget for these policies has risen from millions to billions of reais, covering a large part of the population. However, it is important to highlight the difficulties they face, especially with regard to the inclusion of society in the construction of these policies, since the social reality is one of extreme poverty with even greater difficulty in participation, since social and institutional organisation is weak or non-existent in these places.

There have also been advances in the conception of these policies, since at first the possibility of the endogenous development of the territories was adopted, relieving the state of the responsibility of dynamising them so that they would emerge from a situation of underdevelopment. The aforementioned policies have a proposal for intense state participation in different demands, such as education, production, training, among others. However, it has not yet been able to mobilise territorial society around productive projects that would make one of the objectives of these policies viable, which is to promote endogenous development.

The main objective of this work is to analyse the profile of the actions carried out by the policies implemented, especially through the latest federal government programme, Territories of Citizenship, in order to see if they provide the means for the development of depressed territories. The specific objectives are to map the volume of government resource transfers to the territories, to identify different demands according to the profiles of the selected territories and to check whether the local reality has been a parameter in the decision to allocate resources.

The work is therefore structured in three chapters, in addition to this introduction and the final considerations. The first chapter covers some basic concepts on the chosen topic, starting with a theoretical approach to territorial development. The second takes a look at decentralised public policies for rural development, differentiating those of a more interventionist nature from the previous ones. These two chapters set out to explain how decentralised public policies came about, the international and national context, their theoretical contribution and their progress, specifically in relation to rural development. The third chapter analyses the Citizenship Territories Programme implemented in 2008, using data and information from the Citizenship Portal (www.territoriosdacidadania.gov.br), which lists the social policies implemented in each territory and the resources allocated to them, the Ministry of Agrarian Development Portal ((www.mda.gov.br) and the Territorial Information System http://sit.mda.gov.br). This system provides a characterisation of all the rural territories targeted by public policies.

Through this evaluation in the third chapter, the aim is to see whether this programme provides the basis for promoting development in depressed territories and whether it respects the theoretical framework that supports it. Therefore, the aim is to point out the potential and limits of policies that use a territorial approach and induce socio-productive arrangements, represented by the Federal Government's main programme in recent years.

CHAPTER 1

TERRITORIAL DEVELOPMENT

The liberal hegemony was broken after the Crisis of 1929, when Keynesian theory was strengthened by the great economic recession that persisted throughout the 1930s. The high levels of unemployment, the drop in production and the fall in stock market prices legitimised state action to minimise the effects of the Great Depression.

After the Second World War, developmentalist ideas still persisted and had two main schools of thought, the Anglo-Saxon and the Latin American, represented by Cepaline authors. Both thoughts shared the same means of overcoming underdevelopment, the latter through a closer approximation to a model that had proved efficient as a driving force for development, the capitalist process of industrialisation. In this way, a model of industrialisation was imported from the advanced countries, with a strong national state.

During the golden age of capitalism, after the Second World War, a large part of developmentalist policies were applied, because at that time this ideology was necessary to maintain the systemic order. This was due to the socialist threat, in the context of the Cold War, whose alternative system to capitalism aimed to achieve good living conditions for members of society and advances in economic growth.

The disparity between the social conditions of the countries in the capitalist bloc needed to be explained, since there were national economies that were at a much lower stage of development than the main economies of that period. Furthermore, and more importantly, it had to be shown that these historical conditions were circumstantial and could be changed if certain economic and development policy actions were carried out at national and supranational levels.

In the 1970s, developmentalist policies were judged to be incapable of solving the problems of economic growth and income distribution, as this period saw a crisis characterised by a combination of low growth rates and high inflation rates, a phenomenon that became known as stagflation. In this context, at the end of the 1980s, the neoliberal ideology emerged, strengthened by the fall of the Berlin Wall in 1989, which represents an important historical milestone, the dissolution of the Soviet bloc.

Over the last decade of the 20th century, the process of globalisation intensified and, along with it, the decline of the nation state as an institution for coordinating and leading strategic development decisions. Supranational spaces were consolidated through the formation of regional blocs and the redefinition of the role and power of multilateral organisations, which began to dictate global agendas, exposing the "good" policies and institutions to be followed in order to achieve development.

These "good" policies are expressed in the Washington Consensus instituted in 1989 by the IMF, the World Bank and the US Treasury Department. These policies include reducing public spending, tax reform, market interest rates, market exchange rates, trade openness, unrestricted foreign direct investment, privatisation of state-owned companies and services, deregulation of the economy and labour laws and, finally, the right to intellectual property. This became official IMF policy in 1990 and was prescribed to promote macroeconomic adjustments in underdeveloped debtor countries, especially in Latin America.

Therefore, the Washington Consensus represents the consolidation of the neoliberal vision, laying the foundations for the state to lose its economic policy instruments and establish its minimal role. As Carcanholo (2004) points out, neoliberal reforms are justified as a means of integrating into the international economy and as inevitable to the globalisation process.

> [...] Given this context, nations should implement policies that guarantee their respective insertions, by opening up their economies to a greater degree and deregulating their various markets. This is how neoliberal policies are justified by their advocates. The natural and inevitable development of markets, within a global context, would have created a reality in which the only way for national and regional economies to insert themselves would be through the deregulation and liberalisation of their markets and the reduction of state participation in the economy (CARCANHOLO, 2004, p.283).

Generally speaking, it can be said that the debate on economic development, in the sense of post-war theories, acquired a secondary role in the global debate from the 1980s onwards. This is because the policies defended by this economic development were essentially linked to strong action by the national state, which is not consistent with the neoliberal perspective.

In the 1990s and 2000s, the themes of local development and territorial development gained ground in the discussion about development possibilities. These theories, depending on how they are implemented, have an ideological content that is highly linked to the neoliberal perspective, when they dismiss the presence of the national state in order to achieve development.

From this neoliberal perspective, the local scale is combined with the global scale, with the theoretical and political subordination of the national scale, in which the role of the state is very well defined as merely guaranteeing stability or providing the basis for the regulatory functioning of the market, nothing more. According to this perspective, the local level has acquired strategic importance for achieving national development. Local governments (on a sub-national scale) would be in a position to attract companies and promote their competitiveness. They also offer a solid historical and cultural basis for the integration of individuals, and therefore have a greater capacity for representation and legitimacy with regard to those they represent, given the proximity between rulers and citizens.

Just as neoliberal ideology maintains, a large part of the theories that use the approach to local development see globalisation as something inexorable and irreversible, which would tend to break the limits of national state control, structurally weakened both by the advance of the supranational space and by funding difficulties. Development policy can no longer typically be the product of public state action, but the result of the convergence of actions by multiple actors, some of them acting in the private or supranational spheres.

From a different perspective, a certain current of territorial development, unlike the theory of endogenous growth defended by the current order and "legitimised" by multilateral agencies, explains that the territory is a new unit of reference for the state to act and apply its policies. In this way, it is possible to act in a way that combines multiple scales, since local governments that are not in line with a national project are doomed to failure and interaction between them is necessary.

1.1 Decentralisation and a Territorial Approach

The local development approach gained prominence after the emergence of the globalisation process at the end of the 20th century. Previously, in the post-war period, nations and multilateral agencies had created an environment favourable to different ideas for overcoming the economic crisis and the political and social problems experienced in recent decades, such as the Soviet revolution, the crisis of the 1930s, the Second World War and the Cold War. At this time, the notion of development gained ground and Keynesian postulates were once again discussed in an attempt to remedy the regional inequalities of nations; it was then a time of centralisation of power.

With the intensification of the globalisation process, the discussion of development needed to adapt to an economy and society that had become flexible and decentralised. In this way, the notion of development moved away from Keynesian perspectives, with the logic of the mainstay prevailing and the state having to reduce its role.

Possible consequences of this process, such as the so-called elimination of national borders, the reduction of state intervention in economic dynamics, the increase in the flow of people, the homogenisation of consumption and human behaviour, create the erroneous idea of de-temporalisation, an "end of delimited territories". According to Haesbaert (2006), such de-temporalisation would be the construction of new bases that adopt different and new concepts about territories.

> [...] we defend the idea that much of what the authors call deterritorialisation is actually the intensification of territorialisation in the sense of a 'multi-territoriality', a concomitant process of destruction and construction of territories mixing different territorial modalities (such as 'zone-territories' and 'network-territories'), on multiple scales and new forms of territorial articulation (HAESBAERT, 2006, p. 32).

Among the possible new forms of territories mentioned by Haesbaert (2006), network-territories can be described as articulations between discontinuous spaces of different scales; and territory-zone, continuous spaces of a scalar dimension that constitutes it, as defined by Schneider and Tartaruga (2006). These conceptual innovations are a consequence of the globalisation process, in which the national scale is no longer so relevant, so these new concepts combine multiple scales between the local and the global, but this idea can wrongly distort the non-existence of a supranational hierarchy, made explicit by multilateral agencies and their recommendations.

This highlights the shift in public actions from strong national/weak local to weak national/strong local, and it is then up to the local sphere to promote the overcoming of underdevelopment. In other words, this is when top-down planning (characterised as a top-down policy, i.e. the federal sphere concentrates decisions and relays them to the state and municipal spheres) lost ground to button-up planning (bottom-up policies, i.e. the local spheres - public and private - are the decision-makers), which can clearly be characterised as a decentralisation of public administration.

In view of local peculiarities - social, cultural, economic and environmental - globalisation has stimulated the reorganisation of the political and economic spheres in order to facilitate local development, taking into account the potential and limits of different territories, as Saraceno (1996) points out. This trend has in fact intensified the process of decentralisation in the sphere of public power.

> [...] Each area or region is able to compete better if it is able to integrate historically accumulated local knowledge and skills with information and exchanges with non-local markets. For this reason, the globalisation of markets is more likely to increase territorial differentiation than homogenisation (SARACENO, 1996, p. 17).

The decentralisation of public administration can bring major benefits, such as better information for the government about society and its reality; greater participation by society in the drafting of public policies, which would imply greater policy effectiveness, as this society lives day-to-day with the issues that need to be overcome if development is to be achieved; Increased transparency, since policy-making and implementation would be close to society; increased credibility; the integration of society with the state; the strengthening and reinvigoration of democracy at national level; the reduction of regional disparities; greater attention to socio-cultural factors; the adaptation of development to local conditions, among others.

Through these measures, it is possible to carry out a well-qualified diagnosis, which would guarantee proper policy formulation, because by identifying the territory's own weaknesses and potential, it is easier to draw up precise policies to remedy these weaknesses and exploit the potential. However, it is necessary to emphasise that decentralisation has common misconceptions, as Ortega (2008) has shown: disregarding the macroeconomic environment; minimising the existence of different social class structures; minimising the roles of space and national public policies; the need to take into account history and insertion into the capitalist order.

The most interesting way to promote local development, as Ortega (2008) argues, would be a combination of button-up and top-down policies, since a strong central power is needed to consolidate decentralised policies. The interventionist action of the state aims to inhibit the concentration of power in a certain local elite and to give continuity to policies, preventing short-term political interests from overriding the purpose of policies aimed at overcoming underdevelopment.

> [...] This sets a great challenge: to combine the two forms of planning in order to trigger the development process. From above, with structuring policies for the local reality, and from below, with viable projects, drawn up in a participatory manner on the basis of a territorial pact. All of this, in a context of great complexity of development alternatives, the multiplicity of interests of local subjects, and democratic participation that allows planning to be used as a tool for organising the actions of the state itself (ORTEGA, p. 33, 2008).

In addition to combining the two types of planning, the participation of social actors is essential to guarantee the viability and legitimacy of policies. There needs to be collaboration between the different actors, since in the same place there are different social classes that usually have divergent interests. Therefore, the creation of a territorial pact[1] depends on the willingness to seek common objectives aimed at building development paths between actors from different segments.

Development projects must be built collectively, in concert, with the participation of representative groups and not individuals who may only have personal interests at heart. It is clear that the social structure of the territories is heterogeneous, so allowing projects to be created spontaneously is putting decision-making power in the hands of the strongest and most organised groups. It is therefore up to the state, in its various spheres, to encourage and guarantee the participation of less organised groups, so that the process is legitimately democratic and everyone contributes to the new social process.

There is no one model for development, as it is a process that is built collectively in each territory, covering issues specific to them. This new development proposal stems from the re-democratisation of public spaces, as it articulates state intervention with the active participation of social and political actors, emphasising the need for articulation between the spheres of the state and society as a whole, represented by its groups and institutions.

Graziano da Silva (2002) stresses that in most of Brazil's rural areas there is a weakness in the organisation of social actors, an obstacle that cannot be overlooked. A significant part of the Brazilian countryside is in a situation of extreme poverty, which makes it even more difficult for beneficiaries to participate, as social and institutional organisation is weak or non-existent in these areas. This gap can benefit the best-organised groups, such as employers, which would make it difficult to promote an inclusive development process, as only the interests of a specific minority group would be served, increasingly excluding the poor from public planning decision-making processes.

It is now important to define the concept of territory, as this term has acquired a polysemic

[1] A territorial pact is when a society with divergent interests makes a pact of common interest to promote territorial development, in this way different social classes agree on certain points for the benefit of all.

character. We have adopted Abramovay's (2003) perspective of territories:

> [...] territories can be defined as places of interaction between human societies and ecosystems. Territory is the way in which a given society organises itself in its relationship with nature. This organisation presupposes forms of coordination between social organisations, economic actors and political representatives that are necessarily specific and have a history unique to each place (ABRAMOVAY, 2003, p. 30).

It's clear that the definition of territory involves the relationship between individuals and the space where they interact, through productive activities and sociability itself. However, it is plausible to emphasise that territories are not islands, they are inserted in a national and international context, as Schneider (2003) already addresses in his text: territories have a social, economic, cultural, political or other dynamic that influences the spaces where agents act.

Unifying the contributions of various authors who adopt the same perspective, including Brandão (2007), Haesbaert (2006), Sepúlveda (2003) and Ortega (2008), we arrive at a more comprehensive definition of territory, understood as a delimited space where internal and external relations take place, from a perspective of territorial competitiveness that combines economic, social, environmental and political dimensions. Thus, it is necessary to consider the existence of hierarchies, power asymmetries, social classes, the macroeconomic and international environment, since territories interact with factors exogenous to the locality and internal factors.

For a better understanding of the importance of territorially specific resources, Cassiolato and Szapiro (2003) are relevant. One of these specific resources could be the social capital consolidated in the territory. This term can be defined as the cohesive characteristics of a given population that are passed down from generation to generation, so it cannot simply be transferred, as it is a form of social organisation built up in a specific time and space. This resource can be used as an advantageous tool in territorial development, as it facilitates coordinated actions, but high social capital does not imply automatic development. In territories where there is not a high level of social capital, it is possible to stimulate a culture of cooperation in order to achieve social organisation.

> [...] territoriality is linked to specific interdependencies of economic life and cannot be defined merely as the location of economic activity. It is much more, in the sense that it is linked to the dependence of economic activity on territorially specific resources. Relationships of geographical proximity thus constitute valuable specific assets insofar as they are necessary for the generation of spillovers and positive externalities in an economic system. An activity is fully territorialised when its economic viability is rooted in assets (including practices and relationships) that are not available elsewhere and that cannot be easily or quickly created or imitated in places that do not have them (CASSIOLATO and SZAPIRO, 2003, p.40).

A pragmatic example of endogenous development and social construction of the market is

Third Italy. This territory is made up of Marshallian industrial districts[2] , which have industrialised due to their internal dynamics. Located in the central and northern regions of Italy, around 60 to 100 industrial districts sprang up during the 1980s which, despite being small production units and therefore disadvantaged in terms of their marketing structure, productive scale and access to credit, provided good results.

The success of such districts is attributed to socio-cultural characteristics, i.e. values and institutions in symbiosis with a development process specific to small businesses. Bagnasco (1999) explains the importance of local characteristics in terms of technical skills and management capacity, among others, for the success of local development, as Third Italy has achieved. The harmony between individualism and community solidarity is fundamental to the success of productive complexes like this. The reproduction of this model is not guaranteed, as each location has its own regional particularities, be they social or cultural.

> [...] Capital formation, management skills, technical qualifications, mutual trust and a good social climate are decisive resources, whatever the type of development; their widespread availability, with its own characteristics, is essential for the multiplication of small businesses that some regional and local societies have been able to promote, while others have not (BAGNASCO, 1999, p. 39).

Locational factors are therefore decisive and unique in defining a territory. They can also be advantageous differentials in relation to other territories, as they have their own characteristics that cannot be copied, which can imply a competitive advantage. In this sense, Veiga (1998) states that the localities that are best able to develop are those that have the greatest capacity to generate endogenous factors, directing them towards strengthening social organisation and increasing local autonomy. It is clear that it is difficult for poorly developed territories, which do not have differentiating factors such as high social capital, to develop endogenously and autonomously; strong state action is needed to promote development.

Encouraging the formation of local/territorial socio-productive arrangements[3] is an important tool for promoting development, especially in depressed territories[4] . This can be done by fostering a more cohesive social organisational culture, so as to create more favourable conditions for

---

[2] Marshall demonstrates that the advantages, or at least some of them, of large-scale production can be obtained by a large number of small companies, concentrated in a given territory, specialising in their stages of production and using a single local labour market.

[3] According to Ortega (2008), socio-productive arrangements are the consolidation of private governance structures, also territorially based, which coordinate production chains to increase their scale, with a view to being more competitive in the most dynamic national and international markets.

[4] According to Ortega (2008), depressed territories are made up of municipalities with low levels of development, growth rate and development potential. Their social indicators (education, health and mortality) lag behind the national average, as does their institutional capacity (assessed by the degree of local participation in their management, their financial and managerial capacity).

overcoming conflicts and building a consensus that makes a territorial pact for development viable.

However, even with the incentive to form socio-productive arrangements, depressed territories need strong state participation, along with social cohesion. These territories are not capable of generating endogenous and autonomous development, given their low levels of development, so it is up to public investment to meet the needs of infrastructure, training, financing, land deconcentration, etc. Boosting the economy will only be viable if the necessary infrastructure is in place, if society is prepared to act together, in accordance with the territorial pact, which presents challenges because it is made up of different classes with different interests, and also before investing in the production system, the population of that community must have access to food, education and health, which are basic rights

1.2 The New Rural and Territorial Development

Moving on to formulating the concept of rural territory, the same concept of territory is used, but the new concept of rural must be added. Rural areas were first classified as the sector that was essentially dedicated to agricultural activities, generally associating the term rural with backwardness and the term city with progress. Classic authors such as Marx and Weber categorised urban and rural spaces according to the conflict between these two distinct social realities, in the sense that the former represented the emergence of capitalist forces and the latter the backward feudal heritage.

This assessment is no longer valid, since rural areas now incorporate various production and service activities that are directly integrated with industry, but retain some specific characteristics, such as lower population density, less artificialisation of the environment and a greater weight of natural factors. There is therefore a process of "urbanisation of the countryside" that goes beyond the traditional urban-rural dichotomy. The rural environment is thus seen as a heterogeneous and complex space, and not restricted to the agricultural sector. Legally, in Brazil, everything that is outside the urban perimeter is still identified as rural; there is therefore a need to adapt the law to reality, because, as Graziano (1996) emphasises, the rural environment does not only involve typically agricultural activities:

> [...] the Brazilian countryside has become urbanised in the last two decades (1980s and 1990s), as a result of the industrialisation of agriculture on the one hand and, on the other, the overflow of the urban world into what was traditionally defined as a rural area. As a result of this twofold transformation process, agriculture - which could previously be characterised as a relatively autonomous productive sector, with its own labour market and internal balance - has become integrated into the rest of the economy to the point where it can no longer be separated from the sectors that supply it with inputs and/or buy its products. We've already had the opportunity to show that this integration ended up being consolidated in the so-called "agro-industrial complexes" which began to account for the very dynamics of the agricultural activities linked to them (GRAZIANO, 1996, p. 217).

During the 1980s and 1990s, agricultural specialisation took place, which made it possible to integrate rural areas with industry, forming agro-industrial complexes[5] . This led to a gain in productivity, where the same amount of labour time was no longer needed to produce the same amount. As a result of this gain in "surplus time" in rural areas, conditions were created to carry out other non-agricultural rural activities, and it is in this context that goods and services activities emerged in rural areas, which have become important for generating employment and income for the rural population (ORTEGA, 2008).

Recent transformations in rural areas, especially the increased importance of non-agricultural rural activities, require a new approach to public policies aimed at developing these areas. In this way, agricultural development is not synonymous with rural development; a rural development policy must include planning for the new non-agricultural dynamics, since they are already a reality in rural areas. The incorporation of these activities can be intended to complement income or even to be the sole source of income.

Rural areas have latent local specificities, such as power asymmetry and social and regional inequalities, which are the result of a historical process in Brazilian society. To this end, the territorial approach is an important key to formulating public policies, as it manages to adapt national policies to regional peculiarities within an inter-municipal territorial framework. The creation of inter-municipal socio-productive arrangements is an effective tool for promoting local development, as it is able to maximise the competitive advantages acquired, given the social proximity that is specific to that particular locality.

It is therefore necessary to seek political articulation between municipalities so that a territorial pact can be created to promote local development. As Abramovay (2003) points out, activities in rural areas are based on social relations between a multitude of different actors, and the technical and capital integration of agriculture with industrial and service segments makes it difficult to create a democratic space in the territories. The asymmetry of power needs to be managed so that local elites don't appropriate public policies for the purpose of self-promotion, as has historically been the case.

> [...] In the rural environment, the notion of territory acquires a double importance: firstly, it invites reflection on development to turn to a varied set of protagonists and thus overcome a strictly sectoral scope. The diversification of rural economies is therefore the most important result of territorial development in areas that are not densely populated (ABRAMOVAY 2003, p. 32).

Knowing these factors, rural territorial development policies still have to take into account that

[5] Agro-industrial complexes can be translated into the integration of agriculture with other branches of industry, transforming it into a link in a chain where, on the one hand, there are the industries that supply agriculture with inputs, machinery and equipment (upstream sector) and, on the other, the industries that classify, process and/or industrialise agricultural raw materials, as well as their distribution (downstream sector), thus forming the cycle of industry - agriculture - industry, with one being indispensable to the other for the complex to function effectively.

the "new rural" is inserted in an increasingly competitive environment, followed by intense technological innovations that directly influence competitiveness, but competitiveness is a systemic phenomenon and depends on the territories. External demand also exerts a decisive force on territorial productive transformations, as territories are inserted into a global market. In order for these policies to bring about productive and institutional changes, it is necessary to broaden the concept of the rural beyond agriculture and to value the heterogeneity of territories, which brings different potential to each one.

CHAPTER 2

THE BRAZILIAN EXPERIENCE IN PUBLIC POLICIES WITH FOCUS ON TERRITORIAL DEVELOPMENT

During the military governments in Brazil, a series of rural development programmes were implemented aimed at agricultural modernisation, which would be achieved through the productive restructuring of agriculture and the absorption of new technologies. In this way, there would be a significant increase in production, which would bring with it a "natural" increase in family income, thus achieving the objective of the policies, i.e. "rural development". However, this productivist ideology resulted in experiences that were passively criticised, for example, at the end of the 1970s, there was little significant change in the reduction of rural poverty.

Decentralised public policies emerged in Brazil after 1988, when the new Federal Constitution was promulgated, because its principles included administrative and political decentralisation. This principle differs completely from the dictatorial period, when the state at federal level was strengthened in comparison to the other levels, particularly with regard to the concentration of power and resources. Thus, it can be seen that the state reforms directly affected the entire set of public policies of that period.

The proposal for decentralised development gained ground throughout Latin America mainly due to the strong deregulation of the economy that took place in 1990, when neoliberalism was consolidated and increasingly reduced the state's participation in the economy. In this context, international multilateral agencies (WB, IDB, IFAD, IICA, ECLAC, among others) acted as incentives for neoliberal policies; in the background, the decentralisation process took place due to the strengthening of local forces in the struggle for re-democratisation in these Latin American countries (ORTEGA, 2008). The World Bank's encouragement can be seen in its 2001 documents, a fragment of which follows:

> [...] The combination of increased decentralisation and the development of local democracy are key elements to progressively create the conditions for greater participation and accountability at the local level (WORLD BANK, 2001, p. 13).

At first, during the Fernando Henrique Cardoso (FHC) administration, decentralised policies for rural development began to be developed, with a process of decentralisation in the sense of municipalisation, i.e. not appropriating the inter-municipal approach characteristic of the territorial approach, along with the broader notion of territory. This construction was fuelled by the intensification of agrarian conflicts and the strengthening of the Landless Rural Workers' Movement (MST).

PRONAF was created in 1996, and its Infrastructure and Services credit line required the creation of Municipal Councils for Rural and Sustainable Development (CMDRS), whose responsibility was to promote the political articulation needed to promote local development, in accordance with the Municipal Plan for Rural and Sustainable Development (PMDRS). In 1999, the Ministry of Agrarian Development (MDA) and the National Council for Sustainable Rural Development (CNDRS) were created, and it was up to the latter to set the objectives, guidelines and targets for various programmes. During the FHC government, other programmes aimed at rural development were created, such as the Local Development Forums. Thus, the attention given to rural areas is growing.

Subsequently, an innovative concept emerged, that of the territorial cut-off point. Working with decentralised public policies and the notion of a territory-zone requires the cooperation and participation of all social segments so that the wills of local economic and political forces are not superimposed on those of the less powerful classes. The social segment includes companies, government representatives, trade unions, associations, individuals and others. The central idea behind the inclusion of society is to democratise public decisions and bring the local reality closer to the demands made by state policies for the development of territories, so that, through the local dynamic itself, underdevelopment can be overcome according to its capabilities.

A development project for a territory-zone works on an inter-municipal basis, which benefits the exploitation of comparative and competitive advantages. However, in order for this to happen in a positive way, it is first necessary to organise political coordination between the municipalities, with a view to developing the territory as a whole. This requires the construction of a territorial arrangement capable of identifying the main problems encountered in the region, with the aim of drawing up and finding ways to implement a plan that focuses on overcoming them.

Policies with a territorial focus have been used more intensively and from an inter-municipal perspective in Brazil since 2003, i.e. at the start of the Lula government. This is an option for the development of municipalities with a rural profile and, above all, with a predominance of family farming. Contrary to the mainstream theory of the last decade, territorial development strategies increasingly require state intervention. To this end, decentralisation does not mean that the state has to withdraw from the economy; rather, from this perspective, the territorial cut-out becomes yet another scale of state action (Shneider, 2003).

> [...] the territory emerges as a new reference unit for state action and the regulation of public policies. It is, in fact, an attempt by the state, understood as a legal and social institution, to respond to the strong criticism it has been subjected to, especially in view of the ineffectiveness and inefficiency of its actions, their high cost to society and the permanence of the most serious social problems such as poverty, unemployment, violence, etc. (SHNEIDER, 2003, p.102).

For this reason, in the first year of President Luís Inácio Lula da Silva's mandate, the Secretariat for Territorial Development (SDT) was set up as part of the Ministry of Agrarian Development (MDA). Its basic premise is to guide the strategies of the ministry's rural development policies. The territorial approach is the centrepiece of this reorientation promoted by the SDT.

The aim of this Secretariat is to find a better way of integrating and bringing together the public policies of the various Brazilian bodies, be they federal, state or municipal, with civil society, around the development of territories where family farmers and land reform beneficiaries predominate. The SDT would have the challenge of identifying and designing territories based on regional similarities in order to promote sustainable development.

Considering that the highest rates of poverty are concentrated in rural areas, the Federal Government, through the MDA and the Ministry of Social Development (MDS), has encouraged the creation of territorial arrangements for development purposes throughout Brazil. These arrangements can be set up through one of its programmes, such as Intermunicipal Consortia for Food Security and Local Development (CONSADs), Rural Territories (TRs) and Citizenship Territories (TCs). The first two were created in 2003, in the first year of Lula's government, and the last in 2008, during his second term.

The aim of all these programmes is to unite municipalities with a low level of development around a territorial development project through the formation of new inter-municipal arrangements, characterised as induced territories. In this way, it is possible to break out of a state of underdevelopment through a dynamic unique to that location, and the entire community involved would benefit.

2.1 Previous decentralised policies: the municipal scale

In 1996, during the FHC government's first term in office, the Office of the Extraordinary Minister for Land Policy was created because organised land struggle movements, such as the MST, were stepping up their occupations and pressing for land reform. As a result, responsibility for dealing with the problem was taken away from the Ministry of Agriculture and placed directly under the Presidency of the Republic. From then on, rural development policies shifted their focus towards maintaining family farming, defined as an agricultural production unit in which property and labour are closely linked to the family (LAMARCHE, 1997).

A large part of family farming in Brazil remained on the fringes of the Green Revolution, was unable to appropriate the new technologies and consequently, given the intense process of globalisation, lost competitiveness in the market, even at a local level. Family production was going through a process of exclusion and degradation and, in order to deal with these challenges, credit co-operatives, producer associations, diversification of production and increased occupation of part of the family's time in non-agricultural activities were created. However, these mechanisms have not been enough to solve the problem of producer exclusion. These alternatives are valid and can work in a favourable environment that is not in a state of deep underdevelopment.

That same year, PRONAF was launched, a milestone in terms of rural development policies. Its aim was to promote the sustainable development of family farmers, increase their productive capacity, create jobs and improve their income. The programme had three general lines of funding, Training, Infrastructure and Credit, only the last of which was individual (Production Credit), the first two were passed on to the municipality, which showed the municipalist nature of the programme, but it was concerned with territorial development.

The Infrastructure line of financing was intended for municipalities to address structural bottlenecks in order to energise them and achieve local development, but the decision on how to allocate these resources would require the participation of representatives from the main segments of local society. These municipalities were characterised as poor regions with a strong presence of family farming, where the aim was to create an endogenously designed project, i.e. one that family farmers themselves would create.

To achieve this goal, a new political management institution was created to strengthen the decentralisation of public management. Thus, the CMDRS and PMDRS were created, bringing together the participation of society and local government. The allocation of resources passed on to the municipalities was defined by the PMDRS and had to be drawn up by the CMDRS. All municipalities participating in PRONAF had to have a CMDRS made up of at least 50% farmers and draw up a PMDRS.

The PRONAF Credit line, on the other hand, was realised directly between the bank and the producer, so there was no discrimination as to priority regions; it was the release rules themselves that defined the possibility of this financing. Access to this line was conditional on the endorsement of a technical body such as the Technical Assistance and Rural Extension Company (EMATER), impositions by the bank of services that made the loan more expensive, and the reluctance of managers to grant the loan. Added to the limits of this line of financing was the family farmer's fear of getting into debt. PRONAF Crédito also has a series of sub-lines and specific resources for special groups.

Finally, PRONAF Training aims to train family producers and technicians so that they can meet the demands of the community, as well as to better qualify producers in non-agricultural activities so that they can gain a better foothold in markets, craft services and rural tourism. All these actions need to be in line with the PMDRS.

The main problem in terms of participatory management is that the PMDRS and CMDRS, to a large extent, were merely formal in nature, as they are obligatory institutions for the granting of resources. The councillors have no proactive action. This is due to the local reality, in which the municipality feels threatened by delegating this power to farmers; it is also due to the fact that councillors don't understand that they have deliberative power, that they are not mere hunches or that they feel cowed by the presence of representatives from the municipality and technicians. In this way, the councils do not fulfil their role as a space for dialogue between the different segments of society in order to build a "territorial pact" (ORTEGA; CARDOSO, 2002).

In its first year in office, the FHC government created the Solidarity Community Programme (PCS) in 1995. Its aim, in the context of local development, is to combat poverty in such a way that the state does not act as a welfare agency, but rather as an empowering one. The focus of this programme is to empower individuals and their communities in a specific and autonomous way, emphasising that there is an endogenous capacity for development and that it is only the state that can guide them towards this, as Cardoso (2006) emphasises:

> [...] focussing on the needs of the most vulnerable segments, [encouraging] the participation of society in partnership with the government and [emphasising] the strengthening of community social capital were the guiding principles of a new approach to tackling poverty and social exclusion (Cardoso, 2006 p.4).

The PCS would act as a space for dialogue between society and the government; in this space both would build a project together, with a view to local development. The Programme is an attempt to bring local needs closer to public policies; the federal sphere is too large to be able to identify the needs of the different segments of society. Thus, partnerships between the government (represented by ministers) and civil society organisations (companies, NGOs, intellectuals, artists, etc.) were consolidated through the Solidarity Community Council (CCS), which had the task of defining the priority of the basic social agenda, implementing innovative actions (so that, if successful, they could be reproduced in other locations), encouraging the voluntary participation of citizens, NGOs and corporate social capital.

It can therefore be seen that the PCS was neoliberal in nature, as it relieved the state of its power to take strong action and relayed this role to civil society, while also increasingly encouraging the third sector and investment by private companies. The PCS believed that the resources earmarked for social programmes were satisfactory but poorly spent, so there was no need to create new sources of funding. It is important to emphasise that the work of NGOs implies the transfer of public money to them and the investment of private companies in lower tax payments.

The link between the government itself, between all its levels, took place through the Executive Secretariat for Community Solidarity, which was supposed to promote synergy between public policies so that they would have a significant impact on society. In 1999, the same year the MDA was created, the CCS launched the Active Community Programme (PCA), based above all on local development. It would work through the construction of local forums that would draw up their Local Integrated and Sustainable Development (DLIS) projects. This programme would promote participatory development and concern for natural resources in depressed municipalities, based on partnerships between all levels of government and the Brazilian Micro and Small Business Support

Service (SEBRAE).

The programme's priorities were closely linked to rural areas, as activities related to agriculture, improving family farming, agro-industries, tourism, health, basic sanitation, environmental management and educational programmes predominated. The success of the DLIS depended essentially on the environment in which the locality was located, so it was necessary to have a significantly strong social capital, a space favourable to entrepreneurship and generating income. It was therefore important to invest in human capital, in line with the social capital that already existed. The goal for this programme was for it to cover around 1,000 municipalities, but by 2002 it had only been implemented in 696 municipalities.

The PCA has not fulfilled its objective of boosting local economies, which can be explained by one of the principles of its Programme: in it, the state is only responsible for creating legal and institutional environments favourable to autonomous development. Localities such as those targeted by the Programme are at a level of poverty and underdevelopment that require more than just legal and institutional spaces, they need strong intervention, because they don't even have the infrastructure.

In 1999, the government created the National Council for Sustainable Rural Development (CNDRS), which would deliberate on the National Plan for Sustainable Rural Development (PNDRS). This Council was responsible for drawing up the guidelines, objectives and targets for the programmes: the National Agrarian Reform Programme, the Land and Agrarian Reform Fund - the Land Fund - Strengthening Family Farming and Income Generation in the Rural Sector. In an election year, 2002, the CNDRS underwent a reorientation of rural development and also added two programmes, education and diversification of the economy, as well as intensifying those related to agrarian reform and strengthening family farming.

This reorientation was aimed at local development, and it was the federal government's responsibility to encourage the formation of socio-productive arrangements that would help inter-municipal organisations to exert an active influence on the development of that locality. Inter-municipal organisations can identify the main problems in their micro-region and, in this way , plan development actions that benefit everyone. It is up to the state to encourage initiatives that have the potential to become self-financing in the future and make the micro-region more dynamic, which, without the initial support of the government, would not be able to emerge and prosper.

However, these policies require a strong state presence, not just as a financier, but as an intensive participant in the diagnosis, planning and implementation phases. They were only realised after the end of the FHC government, because the inter-municipal approach to public policies would only be introduced on an ongoing basis during the next government.

2.2 Inter-municipal and territorial policies

In 2003, a series of changes began with regard to rural development policies. These changes were already noticeable at the start of the Lula government, when the Secretariat for Territorial Development (SDT) was created within the MDA. The SDT re-dimensioned the scale of the state's action, appropriating the territorial approach and thus defending the fact that this scale had the potential to bring together organised society and the three spheres of government. The harmony between all those involved in public policies would allow for the joint construction of more effective measures based on the specific needs of each territory. The territories should be made up mostly of rural farmers and beneficiaries of agrarian reform and reorganisation, and it would be up to the government to collaborate in expanding their human and institutional capacities and self-management of the territories.

Decentralised policies are shifting from the municipal to the territorial scale, using the resources previously earmarked for the CMDRSs. The municipal scale is very limited in terms of promoting local endogenous potential, while the territorial scale offers greater social and cultural cohesion due to the proximity of people, social groups and institutions. Thus, based on micro-regional (inter-municipal) identity, it is possible to create socio-productive arrangements that will be key elements in overcoming the condition of underdevelopment.

The SDT identified and set up the rural territories that same year and established some guiding principles for the policies that would be implemented, among them: rural areas can no longer be conceptualised as a sector, as they have incorporated typically urban activities; poverty is concentrated in rural environments and the territorial scale is not detached from the national and international macroeconomic reality, so development is needed with insertion into dynamic markets. In line with these principles, the SDT coordinated the creation of the Intermunicipal Consortia for Sustainable Rural Development, in which context the CNDRS was restructured and renamed the National Council for Rural Development, Agrarian Reform and Family Farming (CONDRAF).

Made up of nineteen councillors appointed by the government and nineteen appointed by social movements and organised civil society, CONDRAF articulates the interaction between society and the state. This Council institutionalises the participation of social agents as protagonists in proposing and managing public policies. To accompany this shift in the scale of public policies, PRONAF's Infrastructure line of financing stopped transferring funds directly to the municipality and instead proposed allocating funds directly to rural territories, as a direct instrument for their development. This change was deliberated at the very first CONDRAF meeting, and also emphasised that this line was aimed at generating an endogenous development process in inter-municipal consortia, rather than improving infrastructure.

However, the great challenge of territorial development is to manage power asymmetries and class conflicts so that the social actors are the protagonists, regardless of how influential they are. This is necessary in order to agree on a common development strategy among all those who make up the territory, and so it is necessary to find a common point of interest. To this end, the SDT was given the tasks of supporting the organisation, institutionally strengthening local social actors and promoting the implementation and integration of public policies. These tasks would be carried out through the following actions: coordination and negotiation of government actions in the territories; support and technical supervision of the territories; planning, monitoring and evaluation of actions; carrying out studies, analyses and training, among others. All of this was aimed at achieving better integration between public policies and civil society.

For the constitution of rural territories, the STD used criteria of social and territorial cohesion and the predominance of rural elements, including small and medium-sized towns. All these criteria are innovative when it comes to delimiting the scale of public policy, these policies should be contained in the Territorial Plans for Sustainable Rural Development (PTDRS), the MDA and the STD officially define territory as:

> [...] a physical space, geographically defined, generally continuous, comprising towns and countryside, characterised by multidimensional criteria such as the environment, economy, society, culture, politics and institutions, and a population, with relatively distinct social groups, which relate internally and externally through specific processes, in which one or more elements can be distinguished that indicate social, cultural and territorial identity and cohesion (MDA/STD, 2005, p. 7).

Currently, 164 territories have been set up, covering 44.93% of the country's municipalities and 28.57% of the population. Unlike previous decentralising public policies, which relieved the state of investment, the TRs are based on the strategy of overcoming underdevelopment through the creation of socio-productive arrangements, in which it is the state's responsibility to invest in basic infrastructure, train social actors and offer official technical assistance, among other actions.

Although the TRs have the principle of overcoming the rural-urban dichotomy, understanding that rural areas have incorporated various urban activities, this is not reflected in their projects. In 2003, only 1.36% of the projects approved were not agricultural or agro-industrial in nature. A large part of the TRs, 73% to be precise, were incorporated in 2008 and 2009 by the Lula government's new Territories of Citizenship Programme, 60 territories for each year mentioned, a second attempt to organise public rural development policies, as will be discussed later. TABLE 1 gives an overview of the TRs Programme, with the total and percentage of municipalities, area and population covered, showing that a substantial part of the policy's target population is covered by the Programme.

TABLE 1 Overview of Rural Territories

	Brazil	Territories	(%)
Number of Territories	164	-	-
Municipalities	5.564	2.500	44,93
Area	8.626.768,60	5.046.045,50	58,49
Population	183.989.711	52.560.160	28,57
Rural Population	28.425.733	15.923.286	56,02
Fishermen	390.676	224.094	57,36
Family Farmers	4.363.034	2.550.151	58,45
Settled families	880.655	645.288	73,27
Social Demand (*)	5.243.689	3.195.439	60,94
Bolsa Família	11.047.139	4.805.853	43,50
Quilombolas	1.467	1.038	70,76
Indigenous Lands	612	340	55,56
Number of High Income Municipalities (**)	1.567	335	21,38
Number of Low Income Municipalities (**)	725	485	66,90
Number of Dynamic Municipalities (**)	1.002	731	72,95
Number of Stagnant Municipalities (**)	2.264	948	41,87

(*)Social Demand: Equals the sum of the Settled Families and Family Farmers variables.
(**)Regional Inequality: cross-referencing the variables "average household income" and "per capita GDP growth". High Income: high household income per inhabitant, regardless of the dynamism observed; Dynamic: medium and low incomes, but with significant economic dynamism; Stagnant: medium household income, but with low economic growth; Low Income: low household income and low dynamism.
Source: Prepared by the researcher with data available at: <http://sit.mda.gov.br/territorio.php?menu=territorio&base=1>. Accessed on: 10/05.

Also in 2003, the Lula government created another initiative that used a territorial approach - the Intermunicipal Consortia for Food Security and Local Development (CONSADs), under the Zero Hunger Programme (PFZ). The aim of these consortia was to help tackle poverty and social inequalities by generating employment and income in food insecure areas. This programme therefore aims to promote "food security", an expression that gained ground in the post-World War II period. At first, it was thought that hunger would be overcome by

exclusively by increasing the food production capacity of the various countries, in other words, by increasing supply.

In 1989, at the 12th World Food Conference, this concept was expanded beyond guaranteeing access to food. It was recognised that poverty was the main determinant of food insecurity and therefore public policies should be aimed at eradicating poverty and inequality so that everyone had access to nutritious food. Supported by this condition, CONSADs aimed to make consumption itself a driving force behind local economies and therefore generate income. CONSADs go beyond the limits of food security welfare policies, as they are based on local development, so that citizens themselves can buy food without depending on the state.

In Brazil, the most worrying region in terms of food insecurity is the northeast: poverty in this region, as in the whole country, is concentrated in regions with predominantly rural characteristics. Based on the 2004 PNAD, around 39.5 million people are in a serious situation of food insecurity, characterised as limited quantitative access to food, with or without living in a situation of hunger.

The PFZ operates in three dimensions: the first concerns structural policies, which aim to guarantee income for the population by generating employment, intensifying agrarian reform, formalising workers, simplifying the process, expanding Bolsa Escola, Minimum Income and encouraging family farming. The second concerns specific policies: the food issue, which aims to guarantee food safety, quality and safety stocks; expanding school meals, among others. The third refers to local policies, which provide support for family farming and urban agriculture, popular restaurants, among others. Rural development policies, together with food security policies, are important instruments for overcoming poverty, which is why the PFZ has adopted CONSADs and the Family Farming Food Acquisition Programme (PAA).

The CONSADs functioned as forums for maximum deliberation, with the participation of 2/3 representatives of civil society and 1/3 representatives of the public authorities of the municipalities that made up the CONSADs, whose agreed decisions gave rise to an action plan. The proposed actions were implemented by the CONSADs Supervisory Board, which established partnerships between the government and NGOs and OSCIPs.

This initiative aims to combine top-down actions with bottom-up interventions, balancing the planning of public policies as a way of ensuring the successful development of the territories. Thus, there are two types of projects carried out by CONSADs: national ones, supported by the MDS, such as the construction of cisterns, community and popular kitchens and the PAA, and those that emerge when the action plan is drawn up.

When drawing up the action plan, the territory's competitive and comparative advantages need to be exploited so that development can be achieved through local synergy. For this to happen, members of society need to strengthen collective action and overcome the individualism inherent in the capitalist system. It is therefore hoped that this articulation will result in socio-productive arrangements that integrate the entire commercialisation, consumption and credit process. Local society must feed this arrangement and feed off it, boosting the local economy.

Still with the same perspective of local synergy and the creation of socio-productive arrangements, the Lula government created its most recent programme, TCs, in 2008. Like the TRs and CONSADs, it uses a territorial approach and aims to promote the development of less dynamic territories. This programme used the territories already delimited by the MDA when it set up the TRs, so they are the same, but the TCs only cover 120 of the 164 TRs. In its first year, the programme covered only 60 territories, then added another 60 in 2009 and continued with the same 120 in 2010. The main difference between this and the old programmes is the attempt to coordinate the government's actions; this involves the participation of 22 ministries and federal bodies; given this large number of participants, the volume of resources for this programme is substantially higher than for the others.

The criteria for selecting territories, according to the Territories of Citizenship magazine, are: Human Development Index (HDI); concentration of family farmers and agrarian reform settlements; concentration of quilombola, indigenous and fishermen populations; number of beneficiaries of the Bolsa Família Programme; number of municipalities with low economic dynamism; rurality; Basic Education Development Index (IDEB); Government priorities or policies, such as Mesoregions, CONSADs, the Legal Amazon, Arco Verde, Extractive Reserves and the São Francisco Basin.

TABLE 2 gives an overview of the Programme up to 2010, since, as already mentioned, in its first year, 2008, it only had 60 territories and, from 2009 onwards, this number doubled. Currently, the programme covers 23.23% of the country's population and around 46% of the rural population. TCs also manages to cover a significant part of the municipalities classified as Low Income by the PNDR typology, totalling 62.48%.

TABLE 2 Overview of the Citizenship Territories

	Brazil	Territories	(%)
Number of Territories	120	-	-
Municipalities	5.564	1.851	33,27
Area	8.626.768,60	4.527.695,40	52,48
Population	183.989.711	42.741.272	23,23
Rural Population	28.425.733	13.128.956	46,19
Fishermen	390.676	210.502	53,88
Family Farmers	4.363.034	2.041.552	46,79
Settled families	880.655	587.234	66,68
Social Demand (*)	5.243.689	2.628.786	50,13
Bolsa Família	11.047.139	4.048.303	36,65
Quilombolas	1.467	973	66,33
Indigenous Lands	612	317	51,80
Number of High Income Municipalities (**)	1.567	163	10,40
Number of Low Income Municipalities (**)	725	453	62,48
Number of Dynamic Municipalities (**)	1.002	623	62,18
Number of Stagnant Municipalities (**)	2.264	611	26,99

(*)Social Demand: Equals the sum of the Settled Families and Family Farmers variables.

(**)Regional Inequality: cross-referencing the variables "average household income" and "per capita GDP growth". High Income: high household income per inhabitant, regardless of the dynamism observed; Dynamic: medium and low incomes, but with significant economic dynamism; Stagnant: medium household income, but with low economic growth; Low Income: low household income and low dynamism.

Source: Prepared by the researcher with data available at: <http://sit.mda.gov.br/territorio.php?menu=cidadania&base=2>. Accessed on: 10/05/10.

The Programme's actions are divided into seven areas: Rights and social development; Sustainable Organisation of Production; Health, sanitation and access to water; Education and Culture; Infrastructure; Support for territorial management; Land Actions. Within these axes, 180 actions are planned for 2010, which can be carried out by NGOs, associations or one of the three spheres of government. The volume of resources earmarked for this programme has grown year on year - in 2008

R$9,941,455,154.32 was spent on the 60 territories, in 2009 R$19,379,988,161.66 on the 120 territories and for 2010 R$26,806,901,566.63 is planned. The next chapter will take a closer look at how these funds have been spent, in which regions and in what type of actions they are concentrated.

Unlike the TRs, the TCs articulate a horizontal arrangement within the federal government, represented by the participation of various ministries and agencies. This is an important innovation for the articulation of their actions. With the aim of better integrating the spheres of government, the State Articulation Committees were created to mediate dialogue between the National Management Committee and the Territorial Collegiates, characterising a vertical articulation. The Colegiados Territoriais are made up of members from different spheres of power and social segments. This type of composition is a challenge, as the possibility of reaching a consensus is difficult and therefore requires overcoming.

Following *the* experience of the TRs, which aimed to foster the process of endogenous development based on local economic and social forces and still with little state resources, the TCs seek to increase the role of the state so that the objectives can be achieved. In this context, the programme mixes assistance policies, because it understands their emergency nature, with policies aimed at developing a dynamic specific to the territory, in order to enable social inclusion through work, offering the possibility of emancipating the population, in a second moment, from assistance policies.

It is clear that the programme is based on social participation through local councils, which will first diagnose the specific potentials and limits of each territory and thus identify the latent resources that exist there, i.e. their comparative and competitive advantages. Strategies will be tailored to them and also to their relative condition in the ecosystem, working within a sustainable development perspective and observing their historical conditioning factors and cultural issues. This is not a simple task, as these are depressed territories with a deep level of poverty. However, with strong state action in the areas of infrastructure, stimulating production and social organisation, this task is possible, while also combining emergency social policies, given their low level of development.

CHAPTER 3

ANALYSIS OF THE TERRITORIES OF CITIZENSHIP PROGRAMME IN 2008

The aim of this chapter is to see if the measures taken by the Lula government, through the creation of the Territories of Citizenship, make progress towards overcoming the condition of depressed territories, through a policy with a territorial focus and extensive investment coordinated by the state. This answer will be found by analysing the national budget earmarked for the Programme in 2008, checking which types of actions are concentrated nationally and regionally and whether they are in line with local reality. This analysis will be carried out on the basis of the budget data for the Territories of Citizenship Programme, based on the 2008 data available on the Transparency Brazil website.

3.1 The Programme Implemented in 2008

In its first year, the Territories of Citizenship Programme involved 60 territories spread across all regions of Brazil, but 48% of them were concentrated in the Northeast, 22% in the North, 13% in the Southeast, 10% in the Midwest and 7% in the South. This concentration in the Northeast is justified by the criteria used to select the territories, since it is mainly in this region of the country that the lowest HDI, family farmers and agrarian reform settlements are concentrated, as well as the number of beneficiaries of the Bolsa Família Programme and municipalities with low economic dynamism.

FIGURE 1 shows the 60 territories covered in 2008, which are located in the most depressed areas of each state. Only territory 51 - Das Águas Emendadas - is an interstate territory involving two states and the Federal District, Minas Gerais and Goiás. Despite being located in a neighbouring region, this territory has particular characteristics, as it involves a large city like Brasília and at the same time includes small towns in the interior.

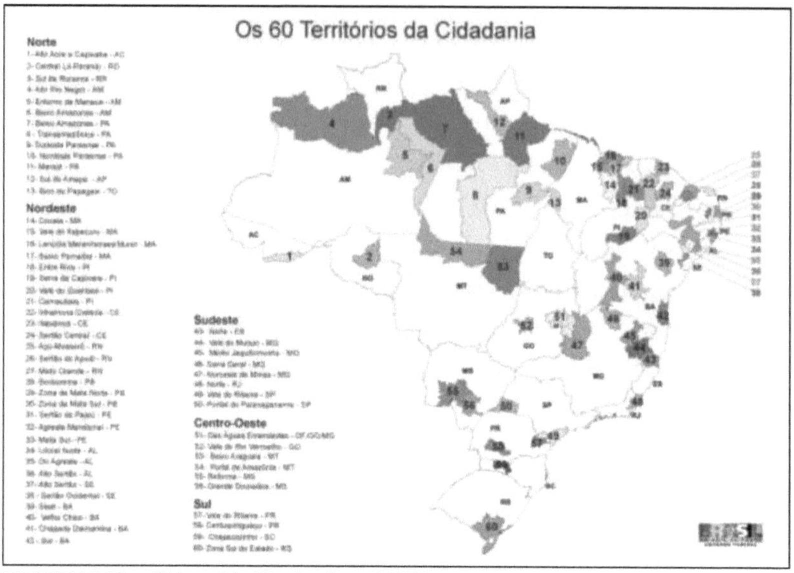

FIGURE 1 The Citizenship Territories of 2008

Source: Available at: <http://www.mds.gov.br/noticias/territorios-da-cidadania-vai-melhorar-a-vida-nas- poorest-regions-of-the-country>. Accessed on: 03/03.

This programme shows the Lula government's self-criticism of the need for investment on the part of the state, since there has been a significant increase in resources and government actions compared to previous programmes of the same government, such as TRs and CONSADs (ORTEGA, 2008). This increase in the Programme's resources came about through the coordination of dispersed programmes under the responsibility of different ministries and federal bodies. This initiative to bring cohesion to the federal government's actions can increase their effectiveness without necessarily increasing the resources allocated to them.

In 2008, the Programme spent R$9,941,298,913.32 on 175 planned actions grouped into seven axes: Rights and Social Development; Sustainable Organisation of Production; Health, Sanitation and Access to Water; Education and Culture; Infrastructure; Support for Territorial Management; and Land Actions. TABLE 3 shows the amount of resources for each axis, followed by GRAPH 1, which shows the proportions spent on each one.

TABLE 3 Executed Budget - TCs in 2008

Rights and Social Development	R$ 4.974.768.837,19
Sustainable Organisation of Production	R$ 1.654.239.821,27
Health, sanitation and access to water	R$ 1.487.533.230,76
Education and Culture	R$ 498.152.416,36
Infrastructure	R$ 1.129.853.780,27
Support for land management	R$ 18.104.857,94

Land Actions	R$ 178.645.969,53
Total	**R$ 9.941.298.913,32**

Source: the researcher.

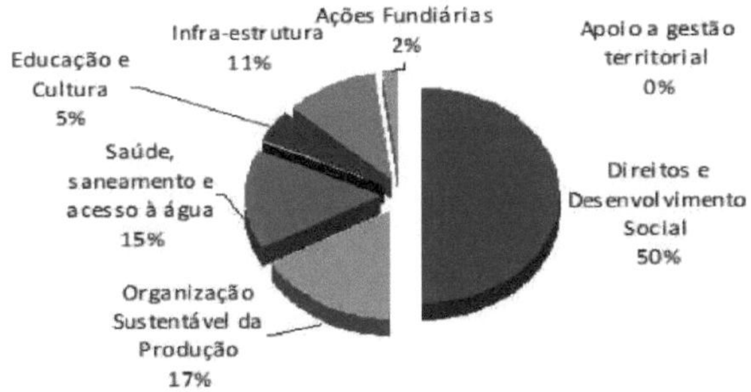

GRAPH 1 Budget implemented - TS IN 2008

Source: The researcher.

It can be seen that the resources were concentrated on actions under the Rights and Social Development axis, and among them the programme that received the most resources was the Bolsa Família Programme. This programme alone accounted for 26% of the total budget allocated to the programme in 2008, totalling R$ 2,545,440,302.61. Another action under this heading that concentrates a significant volume of resources is the Continuous Social Assistance Benefit for the Elderly and Disabled[6] , which represents 23% of all resources, totalling R$ 2,291,157,394.10. Thus, these two actions alone account for 49% of total resources, leaving only 1% for the other actions of this axis such as Specialised Social Assistance Reference Centres (CREAS), Rural Property Registration, among others.

The Sustainable Production Organisation axis received 17% of the programme's resources, 11% of which went to the PRONAF Credit action, totalling R$1,142,554,004.00. This axis, like all the others, had actions planned but not carried out: of the 175 actions planned, 37 were not carried out. Some of the actions under this heading that were not carried out were fundamental to the programme's development strategy, which is based on building socio-productive arrangements, including actions linked to consolidating solidarity economy ventures and supporting, structuring and organising local production arrangements.

Almost all of the actions under the Health, Sanitation and Access to Water and Education and Culture axes were carried out; among the actions carried out, the main ones, in terms of volume of resources, are: Brasil Alfabetizado (Literate Brazil), Expansion of Federal Higher Education

[6] This benefit is intended for elderly or disabled people who do not receive any social security benefit, or benefit from another social security system, and who also have a monthly per capita family income of less than % of the minimum wage. It is a welfare benefit, so it is not a pension.

Institutions, Expansion of Access to Primary Care for the Population of the Territories by means of the Family Health Strategy, Expansion of the coverage of the work of Community Health Agents to the population of the Territories of Citizenship and the São Francisco and Parnaíba Sanitary Sewage Revitalisation Programme.

Around 5% of all resources went to the Luz Para Todos action, totalling R$531,398,419.00; this action belongs to the Infrastructure axis, which received 11% of the Programme's resources. This type of investment is fundamental for laying the foundations for the development of depressed areas, where the local infrastructure situation is precarious. Most of these actions are carried out by the Ministry of Cities and the Ministry of National Integration. The Light for All Programme, in particular, is run by the Ministry of Mines and Energy. Other extremely important actions carried out by this axis are those aimed at land reform settlements, either through credit for the purchase of construction materials or the consolidation of settlement projects. These actions are under the tutelage of INCRA and their importance is justified by the fact that the concentration of settled families is one of the criteria for selecting territories.

The last two axes receive a small amount of funding: Support for Territorial Management and Land Actions. The former is vital for society to understand and incorporate the territorial divide and also to strengthen its organisation, but several actions that were planned were not actually carried out. Therefore, the main problem with this axis is not the small amount of funding, but the failure to implement actions such as Strengthening Associations and Cooperatives and Training Human Resources for Competitiveness. The second axis fulfils almost all of its planned actions and concentrates its efforts on Obtaining Land for Settling Rural Workers, totalling R$ 120,919,345.65, which represents almost 70% of all the funds allocated to this axis.

The distribution of resources can also be quantified at a regional level, to see if there is a concentration of funds in any one region or if they are distributed in proportion to the population covered. Earlier, it was noted that there are a greater number of territories in the Northeast, around 48 per cent of the total, so there will naturally be a greater allocation of resources to this region. As for the regional concentration, this will be verified below with TABLE 4 and CHART 2, which show the total volume of resources allocated to each region of the country and the percentage in relation to the Programme's total allocation in 2008.

TABLE 4 Executed budget - TCs in 2008, by region

South	R$ 638.320.189,77
South East	R$ 1.307.444.012,51
North	R$ 1.628.409.495,74
North-East	R$ 5.435.122.419,39
Centre-West	R$ 932.159.036,91
Total	**R$ 9.941.298.913,32**

Source: The researcher.

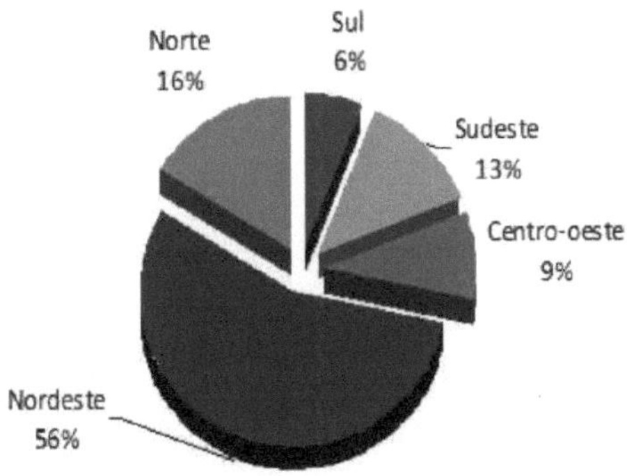

GRAPH 2 Executed budget - TCs in 2008, by region

Source: The researcher.

The allocation of resources should be done according to the level of development of the territories, with those in a more depressed situation needing more resources compared to those in a better level of development. In this way, Kageyama (2004) created a Rural Development Index (IDR), which is the result of a simple arithmetic average of the following indicators: the Population Index (IPOP), the Social Welfare Index (IBES), the Economic Development Index (IDE) and the Environment Index (IMA). The author applied this simple index to the state of São Paulo, distinguishing between high, medium and low levels, according to the incidence of different degrees.

> [...] in general terms, the greater the demographic density, the less isolated the rural areas and the greater the opportunities for establishing social networks; the greater the rural population and its growth over the decade, the greater the capacity of the rural area to retain population; the greater the proportion of people who come from other municipalities, the greater the attractiveness of that municipality in the region (KAGEYAMA, 2004, p. 9).

The result for the state of São Paulo was consistent with its economic and social dynamism: 16.7 per cent of municipalities have a low RDI, a small proportion compared to states in the Northeast. Correia et al. applied this same index to the Northeast and South and found, as expected, a much lower level of development in the Northeast compared to the South. The innovative fact of this work is that, due to its differentiated composition, which takes several factors as determinants of rural development, this index captured a greater number of municipalities in a situation of low development than predicted by the Economic Development Index (IDE); however, the low level of development in the South is still higher than the low level in the Northeast.

Taking the IDR into account, the highest concentration of resources in the North-East region and the lowest in the South region is justified. However, other factors need to be analysed, so a regional characterisation will be made in terms of population specificities and levels of development, to compare with the division of resources there. It will be assessed whether the allocation of resources matches the regional reality and whether it is sufficient to promote development in these depressed territories.

3.1.1 Southern Region

In 2008, the Southern Region had only four territories in the TCs Programme, which were divided between its three states. Traditionally, this region is characterised by its different level of development compared to the rest of the country. This region encompasses 8.6% of the total population covered by the Programme that year and, of the 7 territories selected nationally, 25% fall under the PNDR Typology[7] Stagnant are in this region and none are Low Income. These two typologies are favoured by the state. As this is a more favourable situation in relation to the other regions of the country, allocating 6% of the Programme's total resources to this region is coherent, as its levels of human development in education, longevity and income are also much higher than the national context. FIGURE 2 shows where the 4 territories of the Southern Region are located:

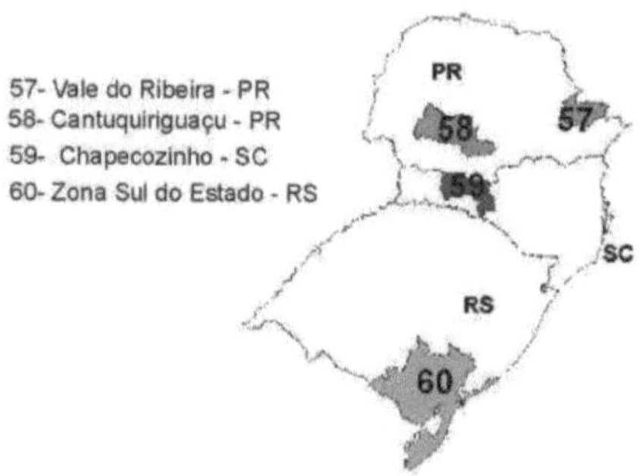

FIGURE 2 Territories Covered by the Programme in 2008 Belonging to the Southern Region

Source: Available at: <http://www.mds.gov.br/noticias/territorios-da-cidadania-vai- melhorar-a-vida nas-regios-mais-pobres-do-pais>. Accessed on: 03/03.

Of the four territories, the one that received the most money was the Southern Zone of the State of Rio Grande do Sul, as it received 51% of the funds for the region and covers 59% of the population targeted by the Programme for the Southern Region. Therefore, there is consistency between the distribution of resources and population coverage for this region, since the other territories received an amount consistent with their population.

TABLE 5 shows the amount of funds spent on each axis of the programme and GRAPH 3

7 The National Regional Development Policy (PNDR) typology aims to establish a reference framework for regional inequalities. Its methodology is based on two variables: the Average Monthly Income per inhabitant, encompassing all declared sources (salaries, benefits, pensions, etc.) and the Geometric Rate of Change in Municipal Gross Domestic Products per inhabitant.

shows the percentage allocated to each axis. There is a concentration of resources in the Sustainable Production Organisation axis. The allocation of resources in the Southern Region differs from the national allocation seen in the previous topic, where the concentration of resources in the Rights and Social Development axis predominates. This result is not surprising, given that the region is predominantly more developed than the rest of the country.

Naturally, when a more favourable situation is found in the territories, the main instrument for boosting them is through actions that help improve production results. Among the actions under this heading, the ones with the highest volume are: PRONAF Credit, Acquisition of Food from Family Farming and the PAA. This region received 16% of all PRONAF resources for the TCs Programme and also allocated its resources according to local demand, whether due to the significant presence of fishermen or settlers.

TABLE 5 Executed Budget - TCs in 2008: Southern Region

Rights and Social Development	R$ 196.642.885,45
Sustainable Organisation of Production	R$ 316.574.410,09
Health, sanitation and access to water	R$ 47.032.953,17
Education and Culture	R$ 15.004.373,79
Infrastructure	R$ 55.747.932,37
Support for land management	R$ 1.049.052,00
Land Actions	R$ 6.268.582,90
Total	**R$ 638.320.189,77**

Source: The researcher.

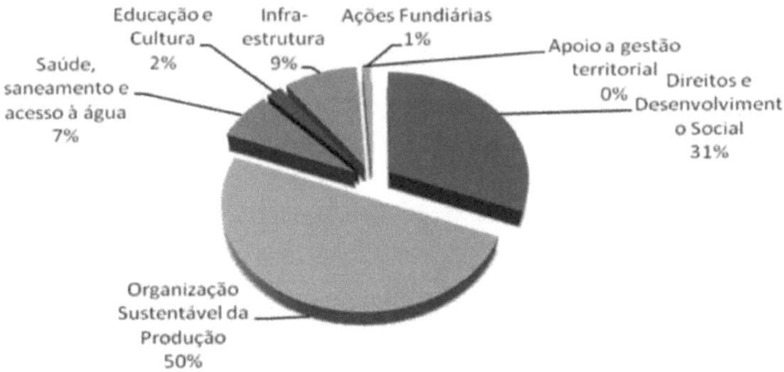

GRAPH 3 Executed Budget - TCs in 2008: Southern Region

Source: The researcher.

Within the Rights and Social Development axis, this region followed the national trend of concentrating its resources on the Bolsa Família (Family Allowance) and the Benefício de Prestação Continuada (Continued Cash Benefit) actions Social for the Elderly and Disabled. As for the other axes, the national trend was repeated, establishing its specificity in investment in relation to production.

3.1.2 Southeast region

The Southeast, like the South, can be characterised by its economic dynamism, which is different from the rest of the country. However, especially in the north of the state of Minas Gerais, there are very depressed micro-regions. This is evidenced by the map of the region, which concentrates the territories in which the TCs operate. For 2008, eight territories were selected for this region, half of which are in Minas Gerais, as shown in FIGURE 3. This region encompasses 12.6% of the entire population covered by the Programme and receives 13% of the national funding. Although São Paulo is the richest state in the country, it is home to depressed territories such as the Vale do Ribeira, which concentrates municipalities with stagnant typologies and low development indices.

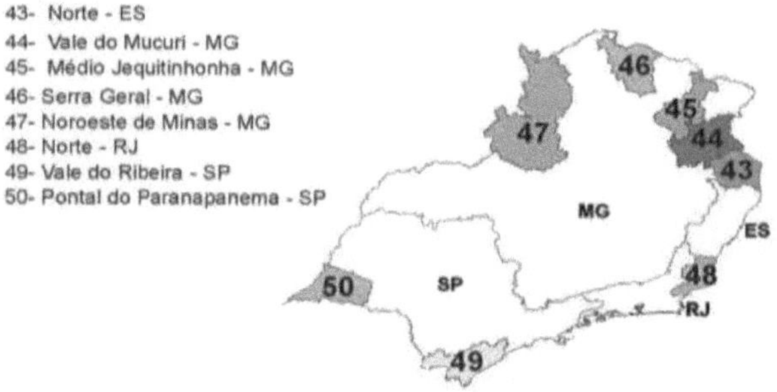

FIGURE 3 Territories Covered by the Programme in 2008 Belonging to the Southeast Region

Source: Available at: <http://www.mds.gov.br/noticias/territorios-da-cidadania-vai- melhorar-a-vida nas-regios-mais-pobres-do-pais>. Accessed on: 03/03.

For the territories in Minas Gerais, the funds spent were much lower than planned, except for the Médio Jequitinhonha territory in Minas Gerais, which exceeded what was planned, while Norte in Espírito Santo and Pontal do Paranapanema in São Paulo also received more funds than planned. This region is home to 20% of the territories classified as Stagnant and 3% as Low Income according to the PNDR Typology. The distribution of resources for this region does not follow the proportionality of the population covered. Initially, it can be seen from the resources earmarked for each territory that the attempt would be to allocate more resources to the territories that are in the most depressed situation, such as those in the north of Minas Gerais, but it can be seen from the distribution of the executed resources that this parameter was not maintained.

TABLE 6 and GRAPH 4 show how resources were allocated according to the Programme's axes, in terms of total amounts and percentages. Like the national trend, this region concentrates its actions on the Rights and Social Development axis, allocating 45% of its funds to this axis. As for the other axes, the region also follows the national trend in resource distribution.

TABLE 6 Executed Budget - TCs in 2008: Southeast Region

Rights and Social Development	R$	579.257.433,96
Sustainable Organisation of Production	R$	264.734.261,97
Health, sanitation and access to water	R$	212.800.110,81
Education and Culture	R$	60.047.305,13
Infrastructure	R$	142.850.107,36
Support for land management	R$	2.371.282,81
Land Actions	R$	45.383.510,47
Total	**R$**	**1.307.444.012,51**

Source: The researcher.

In particular, the territories of Vale do Mucuri - MG and Norte - ES had part of their resources earmarked for the Expansion of Federal Higher Education Institutions - IFES, 7.3% and 5% respectively of the total amount earmarked for the territory. Therefore, part of the Lula government's plan to expand federal universities is being implemented through the TCs programme. In terms of the actions that demanded the most resources, the region follows the national trend, in which Bolsa Família, the Continuous Social Assistance Benefit for the Elderly and Disabled and PRONAF Credit predominate.

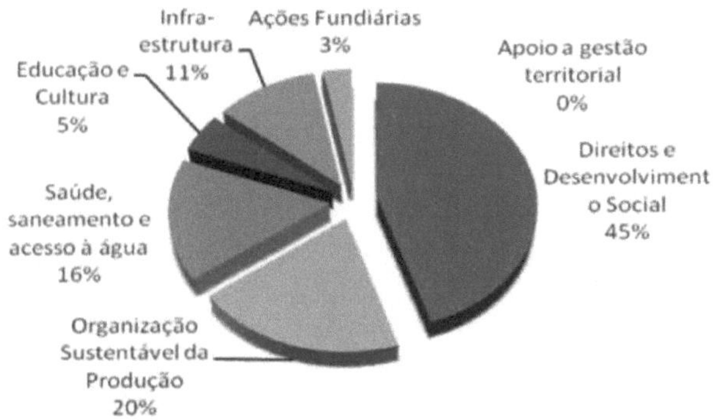

GRAPH 4 Executed Budget - TCs in 2008: Southeast Region

Source: The researcher.

Each territory has its own specific investment needs. It should be noted that the Pontal do Paranapanema - SP territory has the highest concentration of settled families in the Southeast Region, which is why it concentrates 10% of its resources on the action: Technical Assistance and Training for Settlers. The Serra Geral - MG and Noroeste de Minas - MG territories allocate significant portions, around 20% of their resources, to actions aimed at the São Francisco and Parnaíba Revitalisation Programme, which represents 5% of the resources allocated to the region. Still on the subject of territorial specificities, the Médio Jequitinhonha - MG territory allocates almost 45% of its resources to the construction of the Setúbal Dam, i.e. 6% of the region's resources.

3.1.3 Centre-West Region

Located in the centre of the country, sometimes referred to as an economic vacuum, the Central-West Region participated in the TCs Programme in 2008 with five territories belonging to its region alone and one in particular that belongs to two states and the Federal District, the Águas Emendadas territory - DF/GO/MG. This one has some complicating factors, as it encompasses the metropolitan region of Brasilia, so this territory alone receives 47% of the funds earmarked for the entire region, and it covers 71% of the region's population. FIGURE 4 shows where each territory is located, what are consequently the most depressed regions in each state and, in particular, the Águas Emendadas territory.

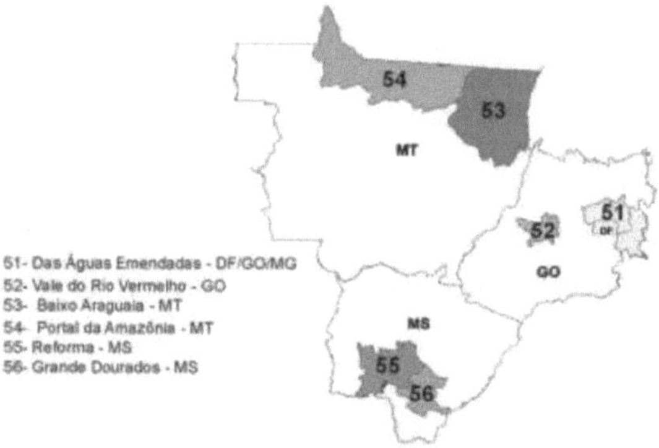

FIGURE 4 Territories Covered by the Programme in 2008 Belonging to the Central-West Region

Source: Available at: <http://www.mds.gov.br/noticias/territorios-da-cidadania-vai- melhorar-a-vida nas-regios-mais-pobres-do-pais>. Accessed on: 03/03.

This region covers around 12% of the programme's target population and receives 9% of the total resources earmarked for it. The distribution of resources is in line with population coverage, but in the territories of the state of Mato Grosso, there is a difference of more than 50% between the resources intended for the territories and what is actually implemented. This region is home to 9.7% of the Stagnant typology territories and none of the Low Income territories.

TABLE 7 and GRAPH 5 explain how the resources were distributed by region, where their actions and resources are concentrated. It can be seen that this region follows the national trend , but differs essentially in that it allocates more resources to Land Actions and less to Health, Sanitation and Access to Water. As only 2 per cent of the national budget is allocated to Land Actions, the region allocates 6 per cent of its total resources and only 9 per cent to Health, Sanitation and Access to Water, as 15 per cent of the national budget is allocated.

TABLE 7 Executed Budget - TCs in 2008: Centre-West Region

Rights and Social Development	R$ 462.412.954,88
Sustainable Organisation of Production	R$ 170.523.721,54
Health, sanitation and access to water	R$ 80.905.978,52
Education and Culture	R$ 60.208.433,26
Infrastructure	R$ 99.142.067,60
Support for land management	R$ 1.674.054,00
Land Actions	R$ 57.291.827,11
Total	**R$ 932.159.036,91**

Source: The researcher.

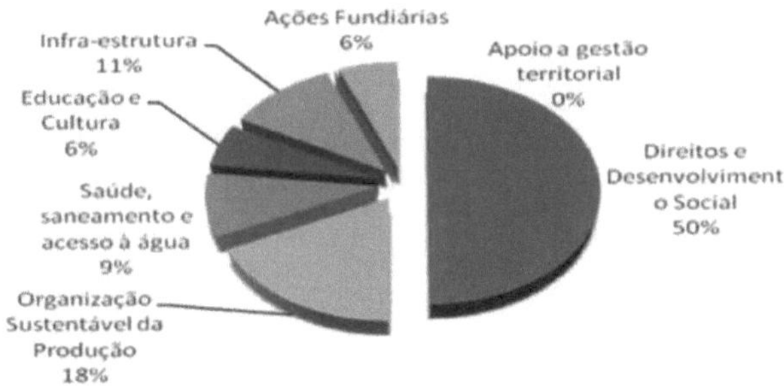

GRAPH 5 Executed Budget - TCs in 2008: Centre-West Region

Source: The researcher.

Among the actions under the Land Actions axis, the Obtaining Land for the Settlement of Rural Workers and the National Land Credit Programme stand out. This region concentrates 14% of the settled families covered by the Programme, so it is not surprising that the Baixo Araguaia - MT territory allocates more resources to the Granting of Installation Credit to Settled Families (Acquisition of Construction Materials) than to Bolsa Família, this territory encompasses 31% of the settled families in the region. This region deserves special attention for actions aimed at the indigenous population, as 16% of indigenous lands are located there, but this is not the case.

3.1.4 Northern region

Thirteen territories were selected for the Programme in 2008 from the Northern Region, which covers a larger area than the other regions, as can be seen in FIGURE 5. This region encompasses 19.4% of the population covered by the Programme that year and 16% of the national budget is earmarked for it. As it is the Amazon Rainforest region, it has more indigenous land than any of the other four regions of the country (62% of the total covered by the TCs). It is also home to 40% of the fishermen and 47% of the settled families covered by the Programme. It is home to 10% of the territories in the Stagnant typology and 18% of the Low Income typology, highlighting the need for massive investment in all areas, as the territories in this region are more depressed than those in the others (except the Northeast).

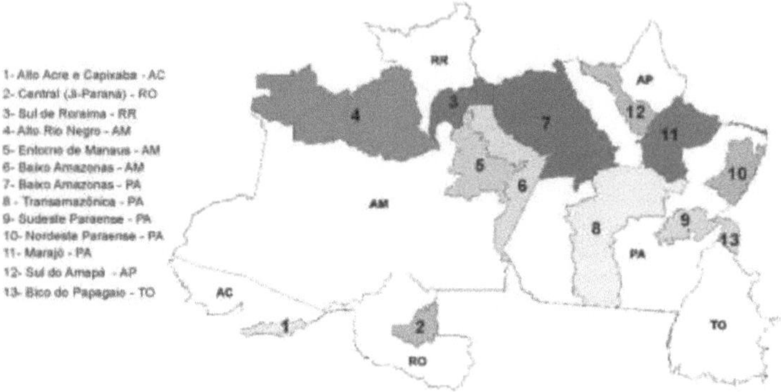

FIGURE 5 Territories Covered by the Programme in 2008 Belonging to the Northern Region

Source: Available at: <http://www.mds.gov.br/noticias/territorios-da-cidadania-vai- melhorar-a-vida nas-regios-mais-pobres-do-pais>. Accessed on: 03/03.

When examining the amount of funds earmarked for the territories of the Northern Region in relation to what was actually executed, it was possible to observe a failure to comply of more than 75% in some cases, such as the Transamazonian territory in Pará, where R$410,914,490.84 was earmarked and only R$92,725,217.95 was executed. All of the territories in this region received much less money than planned, which is unsatisfactory for the development of such a depressed region. This region was R$2,636,901,610.04, but only 60% of this amount was spent on the actions proposed by the programme. This region has a territory that covers a large metropolitan area, which is Manaus and the surrounding area - AM, with a total of 1,980,249 inhabitants, a figure that is very different from the other territories. This territory needs investment in the Infrastructure axis, with typically urban actions such as the PAC/Urbanisation of Slums and Integrated Sanitation and Social Interest Housing. The following TABLE 8 and GRAPH 6 show how resources are allocated according to the seven investment axes of the TCs Programme.

TABLE 8 Executed Budget - TCs in 2008: Northern Region

Rights and Social Development	R$ 873.924.915,64
Sustainable Organisation of Production	R$ 193.372.327,60
Health, sanitation and access to water	R$ 220.612.282,33
Education and Culture	R$ 47.941.707,35
Infrastructure	R$ 260.741.187,72
Support for land management	R$ 4.996.013,50
Land Actions	R$ 26.821.061,60
Total	**R$ 1.628.409.495,74**

Source: The researcher.

The distribution of resources in this region differs from the national level, as it concentrates 53 per cent of resources on the Rights and Social Development axis, while the national figure is 50 per cent. This greater allocation of resources to social policies is justified by the profound state of underdevelopment of the territories in this region. It can be seen that investment in Infrastructure is higher than the national figure, with the region allocating 16% of resources, while the country allocates 11%. Therefore, it can be concluded that there is a very large development gap in this region, and it is up to the state to adopt emergency policies and other basic policies to promote development, in other words, it is necessary to build a foundation so that at a later date it can start investing in actual production. At first, the programme doesn't boost the local economy, but these policies, in line with the local reality, are indispensable for overcoming underdevelopment as the first phase of a larger plan.

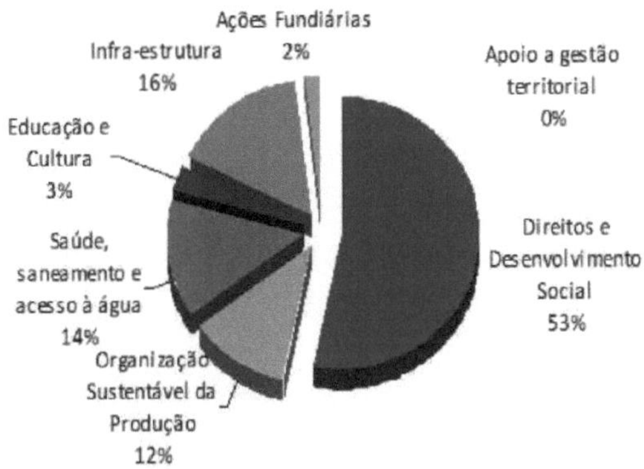

GRAPH 6 Executed Budget - TCs in 2008: Northern Region

Source: The researcher.

The distribution of resources differs greatly between the territories in this region. The territories of Amazonas, for example, allocate only around 3% of their resources to the Sustainable Organisation of Production axis, 70% to Rights and Social Development actions and almost 20% to Health, Sanitation and Access to Water. The territories of Alto Acre and Capixaba - AC and the South of Amapá - AP spend around 25% of their resources on the Light for All Programme, since access to energy is not as easy as in other regions of the country, emphasising their backwardness in relation to the rest of the country and the need for massive investment.

Unlike the other regions, PRONAF Credit does not receive much funding, as these territories are not yet able to support themselves by paying back this type of loan. In the Sustainable Organisation of Production axis, the action that receives the most funding in the most depressed territories in this region is Infrastructure and Services in Rural Territories, while in the more developed or less depressed territories, PRONAF Credit continues to be the action in which the most resources are allocated within its axis.

Given that there is a high concentration of indigenous lands in this region, it would be appropriate for there to be actions aimed specifically at this population. Some were planned, but were not implemented, such as Training in Environmental Education for Indigenous Peoples, Environmental Diagnosis in Indigenous Lands and Implementation, Expansion or Improvement of Sanitation Services in Indigenous Areas. Despite concentrating 62% of the indigenous lands covered by the Programme, only 50% of the funds are allocated to this region and are concentrated in the Rio Negro Territories of Indigenous Citizenship - AM and Manaus and Surrounding Areas - AM, mainly allocated to the Identification, Regularisation and Demarcation of Indigenous Lands action.

Fishermen were not given any specific actions, some were planned but none were carried out, and even though this region includes 47% of the population of this sector covered by the Programme, nothing was done for them. On the other hand, several actions have been earmarked for settled families, with a significant amount of resources; this is consistent with the local reality, as this region is home to 47% of the settled families covered by the Programme. The main actions earmarked for them are: Implementation and Recovery of Settlement Project Infrastructure; Granting of Installation Credit to Settled Families (Acquisition of Construction Materials) and (Initial Support); Technical Assistance and Training for Settled Families.

3.1.5 North-east region

The Northeast Region concentrated 48% of the TCs in the Programme's first year, with a total of 29 territories located in all the states of this region, as shown in FIGURE 6. This region concentrates 55% of the Programme's national budget and covers 47.5% of the population. It is an area characterised by low levels of development and high levels of poverty and income concentration. It is home to 35% of the territories covered by the Stagnant typology TCs and 79% of the Low Income typology TCs, demonstrating its high level of underdevelopment. It is also home to most of the Quilombola communities covered by the programme, with 66%, 62% of family farmers, 49% of fishermen and 32% of settled families.

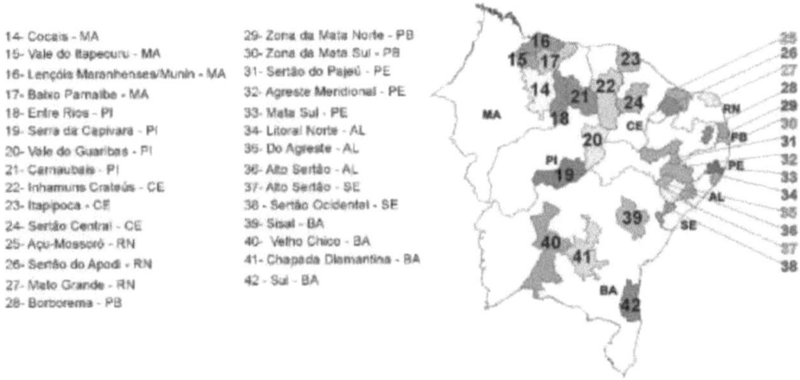

FIGURE 6 Territories Covered by the Programme in 2008 Belonging to the Northeast Region

Source: Available at: <http://www.mds.gov.br/noticias/territorios-da-cidadania-vai-melhorar- a-vida-nas-regios-mais-pobres-do-pais>. Accessed on: 03/03.

The funds earmarked for this region were met in line with the national percentage, with 82% of the region's funds being spent and 81% of the country's funds being spent. Therefore, almost all of the planned resources were spent, with the exception of a few cases such as Cocais - MA, where R$530,292,614.68 was planned, but only 70% of this amount was spent. The Entre Rios - PI territory was the one that concentrated the most resources, and this is justified by its population concentration, which is around 50% higher than the others. The Vale do Itapecuru (MA) territory is the one with the highest concentration of quilombola communities. Four actions were planned for this section of society, but only one of them was carried out, the Recognition, Demarcation and Titling of Remaining Quilombola Areas. It can be seen that the demands of this section of society are not being met, as this territory has not spent even 1% of its resources on quilombola communities.

TABLE 9 and GRAPH 7 show how the region's resources were distributed, the first in total levels and the second in percentage. It's clear that because the region is underdeveloped, it concentrates most of its resources on Rights and Social Development actions, in the same way that they are allocated nationally, but even more so. The Health, Sanitation and Access to Water and Education and Culture axes are allocated larger shares than the national ones, because this region has the worst HDI, so longevity and education levels are below the national average, hence the need for greater investment.

TABLE 9 Executed Budget - TCs in 2008: Northeast Region

Rights and Social Development	R$ 2.862.514.924,95
Sustainable Organisation of Production	R$ 709.282.794,70
Health, sanitation and access to water	R$ 963.781.179,14
Education and Culture	R$ 314.932.971,83
Infrastructure	R$ 533.773.212,01
Support for land management	R$ 7.940.627,00

Land Actions	R$ 42.896.709,76
Total	**R$ 5.435.122.419,39**

Source: The researcher.

The Sustainable Organisation of Production axis receives a lower percentage than the national one, due to the fact that social demands are more urgent than those related to the organisation of production. Similarly, the Land Actions axis receives less than the national percentage, which hinders the process of land deconcentration, maintaining a concentrated land structure, despite the large number of family farmers.

Given the volume of resources earmarked for this region and the fulfilment of a significant portion of what was planned, one can see the government's commitment to trying to develop a region that has historically shown low levels of development. Public policies that try to remedy the great regional disparities, especially in the Northeast (which has not kept pace with the country's development), have existed since the government of Juscelino Kubistcheck, with the creation of SUDENE, based on the developmentalist principles of Celso Furtado.

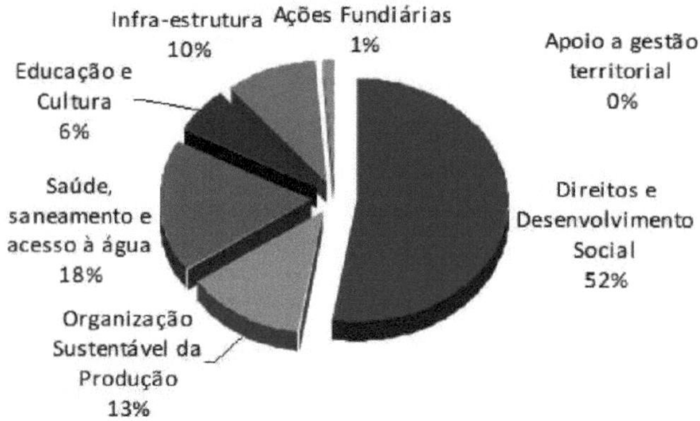

GRAPH 7 Executed Budget - TCs in 2008: Northeast Region

Source: The researcher.

3.2 Analysis of the National Budget allocated to the Territories of Citizenship Programme in 2008

The Territories of Citizenship Programme has a substantial volume of resources, the result of an initiative to coordinate programmes and policies from different Ministries and Federal Agencies. This initiative has made it possible to invest more consistently with the local reality, as these programmes have been dispersed according to the local reality of each territory, organised through the Territorial Collegiate, which has become a space for discussion, planning and implementation of actions. It is in this space that the Territorial Development Plan is defined, strengthening the relationship between society and government.

Analysing each region separately, it became clear that this objective is partially met, as it still has shortcomings in terms of allocation according to social demand. There is a minority share of spending on investments, actions that would strengthen the bonds of society in the sense of associativism, cooperativism, solidarity ventures, actions that would strengthen local social capital and, in particular, the autonomy of its development process. This type of action is essential for the development and consolidation of socio-productive arrangements, which are the main instrument for boosting the economy according to the programme's plan.

The concentration of resources on actions such as PRONAF Credit has its limitations, because access to this type of financing is not simple. The following difficulties in accessing PRONAF Credit stand out: The need for a bank branch to offer this government service, usually Banco do Brasil and Bando do Nordeste. In the case of the Northeast, many managers characterise the programme as uninteresting, since it doesn't bring in much bank business and also requires a lot of work. As a result, the farmer has to deal with the unpleasant situation of the branches being unwilling to offer this resource, as well as feeling inhibited about entering the place with his clothes on. Another important factor is the lack of publicity for the programme, due to the low level of social organisation in rural areas and the fear of indebtedness on the part of the farmer, who fears losing his only asset, the land.

Farmers need to have a regularised CPF and a "clean name", i.e. not have any debts to their name in order to access the loan, but sometimes farming activities don't produce profits but losses, which leads farmers into debt. There is a further complicating bureaucratic factor: the Declaration of Aptitude to PRONAF, which can only be issued by EMATER or the Rural Union, both of which may not exist in some territories.The distribution of resources according to axes of action shows that in regions where the level of underdevelopment is greater, such as the North and Northeast, it is social policies that predominate in state investment. As such, the programme is still at an embryonic stage, where it is unable to boost the local economy due to emergency demands. TABLE 10 shows the percentage allocated to each region in the Programme's seven axes. It is clear that the more dynamic the region, the greater the investment in Sustainable Production Organisation and the less allocated to Rights and Social Development actions.

TABLE 10 Percentage Distribution of the TC Budget in 2008 by Region

	South	**South East**	**Centre-West**	**North**	**North-East**
Rights and Development Social	31%	44%	50%	54%	53%
Sustainable Organisation Org	50%	20%	18%	12%	13%

anisation Production					
Health, sanitation and access to water	7%	16%	9%	14%	18%
Education and Culture	2%	5%	6%	3%	6%
Infrastructure	9%	11%	11%	16%	10%
Support for land management	0%	0%	0%	0%	0%
Land Actions	1%	3%	6%	2%	1%

Source: The researcher.

Also based on the data in TABLE 10, we can see the low level of spending on actions to Support Territorial Management. Since the territorial approach is an innovative policy, it is necessary to train society to incorporate it, and such actions would facilitate the smooth progress of the objective of boosting the local economy. TABLE 11 shows the amount of resources earmarked for the programme and for each region, and what was actually implemented.

TABLE 11 Planned and Executed Budget of the TCs in 2008 by Region and Country

	Forecast	Executed	(%)
South	R$ 654.048.654,00	R$ 638.320.189,77	97%
South East	R$ 1.584.029.115,00	R$ 1.307.444.012,51	82%
Centre-West	R$ 1.315.438.346,00	R$ 932.159.036,91	70%
North	R$2.636.901.610,04	R$ 1.628.409.495,74	60%
North-East	R$6.587.755.444,00	R$ 5.435.122.419,39	82%
National	R$2.256.829.318,00	R$ 9.941.455.154,32	81%

Source: The researcher.

The North and Centre-West regions suffered the most in the planned/executed ratio, hampering the possibility of development in these regions, especially the North, which has a higher degree of underdevelopment than the Centre-West, especially in terms of infrastructure. The other regions had percentages similar to those at national level. It is worth highlighting the South, which, although the amount planned was much lower than that of the other regions, was almost completely fulfilled, which may indicate its society's greater capacity for organisation.

The Programme is therefore assessed positively, but its limitations are still evident in the construction of a development process that strengthens the productive capacity of the territories. There is nothing to prevent these difficulties from being modified in the course of the programme, and the dynamising actions actually taking place to overcome underdevelopment. However, to date, it is the compensatory policy actions that have concentrated the greatest volume of spending.

CHAPTER 4

FINAL CONSIDERATIONS

Public policies with a territorial focus were created at a time of neoliberal hegemony. However, these policies do not contradict the neoliberal prescription, as they recommend the creation of socio-productive arrangements for the autonomous and endogenous construction of development processes. In other words, a kind of release of national states from their obligations towards local/territorial development. In other words, these policies aim to promote the development of depressed territories through their own internal dynamics, stemming from irreproducible local specificities.

The success of the Third Italy region in the 1970s and 1980s served as a reference point for these policies, exemplifying how locational factors can change a stagnant environment into a region with an efficient production system. By valuing the endogenous capacities of territories, the state is exonerated from active participation in the process of dynamising the territory, emphasising its autonomy in promoting it.

Multilateral agencies such as the World Bank, IMF, FAO, IICA and ECLAC, especially for Latin America, began recommending the adoption of such territorial policies. Various seminars and training processes have been promoted to implement this policy, which has an innovative theoretical matrix, focusing on social capital and social organisation with the aim of promoting the development of the production system through socio-productive arrangements. These policies have been adopted by developing countries such as Brazil, Mexico and Chile, among others.

In Brazil, the first policies of this nature were adopted during the FHC government, but their focus was on the municipal level. It wasn't until the Lula government that territorial policies were introduced, following the creation of the SDT within the Ministry of Agrarian Development (MDA) in his first year in office. The policies implemented from 2003 onwards followed the practices recommended by multilateral agencies, low state investment and the assessment that development would be achieved autonomously and endogenously by each territory. However, in the second term of the Lula government, more precisely in 2008, there was a change in the perspective of these policies. It can be concluded that the government was self-critical and realised that greater state intervention was needed to boost depressed territories, and with this in mind, the Territories of Citizenship Programme was created.

It is necessary to emphasise the significant progress that this Programme represents in terms of increased state investment and participation in its three spheres of government. It should also be noted that there has been a continuous increase in the resources allocated to the TCs over the three years of the Programme, 2008, 2009 and 2010.

According to the data on this programme in 2008, the less developed the region, the greater the spending on compensatory policies, as was seen in the North and Northeast, mainly with resources concentrated on Bolsa Família and the Continuous Cash Benefit for the Elderly and Disabled. It was also found that there were few actions aimed at Support for Territorial Management, which hinders the creation of socio-productive arrangements, the main instrument for boosting the local economy advocated by this programme. What is even more serious, however, is the relatively small amount of resources allocated to innovative productive investments, which could better boost the local economy. So far, particularly in the depressed territories, resources have been concentrated on spending on compensatory policies, which shows how difficult it is for these territories to build virtuous trajectories in an autonomous and endogenous way, as the original formulators of these proposals would like, i.e. those who take them as a reference point for a neoliberal model.

BIBLIOGRAPHICAL REFERENCES

ABRAMOVAY, R. **The future of rural regions.** Porto Alegre: UFRGS, 2003.

BAGNASCO. A. Regional development, local society and the diffuse economy. In: COCCO. G.; URANI. A. P. (Orgs). **Entrepreneurs and jobs in the new productive territories**: The case of the third Italy; - Rio de Janeiro: DP&A, 1999.

BECATTINI, G. Industrial districts in Italy. In: URANI, A.; COCCO, G.;GALVÃO, A. P. (org.) **Empresários e empregos nos novos territórios produtivos**: The case of the third Italy; - Rio de Janeiro: DP&A, 1999.

BENKO, G. **Economy, space and globalisation: at the dawn of the 21st century**. 3.ed. São Paulo: Hucitec, 2002.

BRANDÃO, C.A. **Territory & Development. The multiple scales between local and global.** Campinas-SP: Unicamp, 2007b.

BRAZIL. Ministry of Agrarian Development. Available at: <http://www.nead.gov.br>. Accessed on 28 September 2009.

BRAZIL. Ministry of Social Development and Fight against Hunger. Available at: < http://www.mds.gov.br/bolsafamilia>. Accessed on 01 October 2009.

BRAZIL. Ministry of Agrarian Development. **Electronic Magazine "Territories of Citizenship: Integrating Public Policies to Reduce Inequalities".** Available at <www.territoriosdacidadania.gov.br>. Accessed on 20 September 2009.

CAMPANHOLA, C. and GRAZIANO DA SILVA, J. Desenvolvimento Local e a Democratização dos Espaços Rurais. **Cadernos de Ciência e Tecnologia**, Brasília.17(1):11 40 (Jan/Apr), 2000.

CARCANHOLO, M. D. Neoliberalism and Development in a Peripheral Economy. In: CHAVIER, C. L. (org) **Desenvolvimento Desigual**. Uberlândia: Edufu, 2004.

CARDOSO, Ruth. **The new role of civil society in combating poverty and social exclusion.** 2000. Available at: <http://www.iabd.org.br>. Accessed on 15 January 2010.

CORREA, V.P.; SILVA, F.F.; NEDER, H.D. Índice de Desenvolvimento Rural e Políticas Public. Analysing PRONAF releases in the Northeast and South of Brazil. In: ORTEGA, A. C.. **(Territory, Public Policies and Development Strategies.** Campinas: Editora Alínea, 2007.

DEYON, P. **Territorial development: historical context**. France Analyses and Reflections, March

2001. Available at <www.ambafrance.org.br>. Accessed on 26 September 2009.

GRAZIANO DAS SILVA, J. **A Nova Dinâmica da Agricultura Brasileira**. Campinas, Institute of Economics - Unicamp, 1996.

GRAZIANO DAS SILVA, J. **O novo rural brasileiro**. Campinas, Instituto de Economia-Unicamp, 1999.

HAESBAERT, R. **The Myth of Desterritorialisation. From the "End of Territories" to Multiterritoriality.** Rio de Janeiro, Editora Bertrand, 2006.

KAGEYAMA, A. **Desenvolvimento rural: conceito e um exemplo de medida**. In: **Proceedings** of the XLIII National Congress of the Brazilian Society of Rural Economics and Sociology. Cuiabá-MT, 2004.

MDA/CONDRAF. **Guidelines for Sustainable Rural Development**. Brasilia, 2006.

MDA/SDT. **Framework for Supporting the Development of Rural Territories.** Brasilia, SDT Document Series: number 1. March 2005 version.

MDA/SDT. **References for a Sustainable Rural Development Strategy in Brazil**. Brasilia, SDT Documents Series: number 1. Version March 2005.

LAMARCHE. H. (Orgs). **Family farming: an** international comparison. Campinas, Unicamp, 1997.

REIS, J. Globalisation as a metaphor for perplexity? Geo-economic processes and the 'simple' functioning of complex systems. In: Santos, B.S. **A Globalização e as Ciências Sociais**. São Paulo, Editora Cortez, 2002.

ORTEGA, A.C. **Territórios Deprimidos:** os desafios das políticas de desenvolvimento territorial rural. Campinas-SP: Alínea, 2008.

ORTEGA, A.C. Economic development, public policies and rural territorial governance structures. In: Jacy Seixas and Josiane Cerasoli. (Org.). **UFU, 30 years - stumbling across universes** (arts, humanities, sciences). 1 ed. Uberlândia: Edufu, 2008, v. 1, p. 273-300.

ORTEGA, A. C. and CARDOSO, A. Potencial e Limites de uma Política de Desenvolvimento Local: o pronaf à luz do Leader. In: **Revista de Economia e Sociologia Rural**. Vol. 40, n.2, Apr/Jun, 2002 pag.265-304.

ORTEGA, A.C; MUNIZ, A.L.P.; JESUS C.M.; LIMA F.L. **Rural Territorial Development and Intermunicipal Consortia:** policies to induce socio-productive arrangements in Minas Gerais. (mimeo)

SARACENO, E. **The concept of rurality: problems of definition on a European scale**. Rome: 1996. Available at: <http://www.eco.unicamp.br/projetos/rurbano>.

SCHNEIDER, S. **The Territorial Approach to Rural Development and Its External Articulations.** In: 1st International Forum on Territory, Rural Development and Democracy, Fortaleza/Ceará, 2003.

VEIGA, J. E. **Sustainable development:** the challenge of the 21st century. Rio de Janeiro: Garamond, 2005.

VEIGA, José E. **Cidades imaginárias**: o Brasil é menos urbano do que se calcula. Campinas: Ed. Autores Associados, 2002.

VEIGA, José E. The rural face of development. In: **27th National Economics Meeting.** Belém: 1999.

WORLD BANK. **World development report 2000/2001:** Attacking Poverty. Washington: WB, 2001. Available at: <http://www.worldbank.org/wdr/>

MIX
Papier aus verantwortungsvollen Quellen
Paper from responsible sources
FSC® C105338

Printed by Books on Demand GmbH, Norderstedt / Germany